Darkthrone's
A Blaze in the Northern Sky

33 1/3 Global

33 1/3 Global, a series related to but independent from **33 1/3**, takes the format of the original series of short, music-based books and brings the focus to music throughout the world. With initial volumes focusing on Japanese and Brazilian music, the series will also include volumes on the popular music of Australia/Oceania, Europe, Africa, the Middle East, and more.

33 1/3 Japan

Series Editor: Noriko Manabe

Spanning a range of artists and genres—from the 1970s rock of Happy End to technopop band Yellow Magic Orchestra, the Shibuya-kei of Cornelius, classic anime series *Cowboy Bebop*, J-Pop/EDM hybrid Perfume, and vocaloid star Hatsune Miku—**33 1/3 Japan** is a series devoted to in-depth examination of Japanese popular music of the twentieth and twenty-first centuries.

Published Titles:
Supercell's *Supercell* by Keisuke Yamada
Yoko Kanno's *Cowboy Bebop Soundtrack* by Rose Bridges
Perfume's *Game* by Patrick St. Michel
Cornelius's *Fantasma* by Martin Roberts
Joe Hisaishi's *Soundtrack for My Neighbor Totoro* by Kunio Hara

Forthcoming Titles:
Nenes's *Koza Dabasa* by Henry Johnson
Shonen Knife's *Happy Hour* by Brooke McCorkle

33 1/3 Brazil

Series Editor: Jason Stanyek

Covering the genres of samba, tropicália, rock, hip hop, forró, bossa nova, heavy metal and funk, among others, **33 1/3 Brazil** is a series devoted to in-depth examination of the most important Brazilian albums of the twentieth and twenty-first centuries.

Published Titles:
Caetano Veloso's *A Foreign Sound* by Barbara Browning
Tim Maia's *Tim Maia Racional Vols. 1 & 2* by Allen Thayer
João Gilberto and Stan Getz's *Getz/Gilberto* by Brian McCann
Dona Ivone Lara's *Sorriso Negro* by Mila Burns
Gilberto Gil's *Refazenda* by Marc A. Hertzman
Milton Nascimento and Lô Borges's *The Corner Club* by Jonathon Grasse

Forthcoming Titles:
Jorge Ben Jor's *África Brasil* by Frederick J. Moehn
Naná Vasconcelos's *Saudades* by Daniel B. Sharp
Racionais MCs' *Sobrevivendo no Inferno* by Marília Gessa and Derek Pardue

33 1/3 Europe

Series Editor: Fabian Holt

Spanning a range of artists and genres, **33 1/3 Europe** offers engaging accounts of popular and culturally significant albums of Continental Europe and the North Atlantic from the twentieth and twenty-first centuries.

Published Titles:
Darkthrone's *A Blaze in the Northern Sky* by Ross Hagen

Forthcoming Titles:
Ivo Papasov's *Balkanology* by Carol Silverman
Modeselektor's *Happy Birthday* by Sean Nye
Heiner Müller and Heiner Goebbels's *Wolokolamsker Chaussee* by Philip V. Bohlman
Ardit Gjebrea's *Projekt Jon* by Nicholas Tochka
Bea Playa's *I'll Be Your Plaything* by Anna Szemere and András Rónai
Various Artists' *DJs do Guetto* by Richard Elliott
Los Rodriguez's *Sin Documentos* by Fernán del Val and Héctor Fouce

Mercyful Fate's *Don't Break the Oath* by Henrik Marstal
Amália Rodrigues's *Live at the Olympia* by Lila Ellen Gray
Vopli Vidopliassova's *Tantsi* by Maria Sonevytsky
Édith Piaf's *Recital 1961* by David Looseley

Darkthrone's A Blaze in the Northern Sky

Ross Hagen

Series Editor: Fabian Holt

BLOOMSBURY ACADEMIC
LONDON · NEW YORK · OXFORD · NEW DELHI · SYDNEY

BLOOMSBURY ACADEMIC
Bloomsbury Publishing Inc
50 Bedford Square, London, WC1B 3DP, UK
1385 Broadway, New York, NY 10018, USA
29 Earlsfort Terrace, Dublin 2, Ireland

BLOOMSBURY, BLOOMSBURY ACADEMIC and the Diana logo
are trademarks of Bloomsbury Publishing Plc

First published in the United States of America 2020
Reprinted 2021 (twice), 2024 (twice)

A catalogue record for this book is available from the British library

Library of Congress Cataloging-in-Publication Data
Names: Hagen, Ross (William Ross) author. Title: A blaze in the
northern sky / Ross Hagen. Description: New York :
Bloomsbury Academic, 2020. | Series: 33 1/3
Europe | Includes bibliographical references and index. | Summary: "Analyzes
the music of Darkthrone and Norwegian black metal through the lens of exotic
"Northern-ness," exploring black metal's global appeal and commercialization
as a distinctly Scandinavian musical style"– Provided by publisher.
Identifiers: LCCN 2020014178 | ISBN 9781501354328 (hardback)
| ISBN 9781501354335 (paperback) | ISBN 9781501354359 (pdf)
| ISBN 9781501354342 (ebook) Subjects: LCSH: Black metal (Music)–Norway–
History and criticism. | Darkthrone (Musical group). Blaze in the Northern Sky.
Classification: LCC ML3534.6.N8 H3 2020 | DDC 782.42166092/2 [B]–dc23
LC record available at https://lccn.loc.gov/2020014178

ISBN: HB: 978-1-5013-5432-8
          PB: 978-1-5013-5433-5
          ePDF: 978-1-5013-5435-9
          ePUB: 978-1-5013-5434-2

Series: 33 1/3 Europe

Typeset by Integra Software Services Pvt. Ltd.
Printed and bound in Great Britain

To find out more about our authors and books visit www.bloomsbury.com and sign
up for our newsletters.

For Nora and Graham, and my parents,
Bill and Goldie.

Contents

List of Illustrations

Acknowledgments

HAILS to everyone who has contributed in some small way to the years-long journey that ultimately led me to this book; I know I am leaving people out. Special thanks to all of my colleagues in metal studies whose support, critique, and scholarship has been invaluable over the years, especially Deena Weinstein, Jeremy Wallach, and Keith Kahn-Harris. Many thanks to the musicology faculties at Davidson College and CU-Boulder, particularly Neil Lerner and Jeremy Smith, whose mentorship guided my early interests in the field. Thanks also to my indulgent colleagues and students at Utah Valley University. HAILS and AVES to my metal brothers in HERETIC TEMPLE and SPAWN OF THE MATRIARCH. Keep it grim and/ or brutal! Many thanks to Leah Babb-Rosenfeld and Fabian Holt with Bloomsbury who helped immensely in shepherding this beast to fruition. Finally, eternal thanks to all my friends and family, and particularly my parents, whose support and encouragement made this book possible.

Introduction: "Kathaarian Life Code"

For fans of Norwegian black metal, Darkthrone are as much an institution as they are a band. From their beginnings in the late 1980s, they have released seventeen studio albums and several EPs and compilations of demos. The band formed in the latter half of the 1980s in the Oslo suburbs, initially playing death metal and signing with the English independent label Peaceville Records. Their first album, *Soulside Journey* (1990), was a solid death metal album very much in line with the mid-paced death metal that dominated the Peaceville roster at that time. Their second album, *A Blaze in the Northern Sky*, followed in 1992 and marked a radical change in musical and artistic direction, particularly in terms of its unpolished sound. This record ultimately became one of the foundational albums of Norwegian black metal. Darkthrone's following albums, *Under a Funeral Moon* (1993) and *Transilvanian Hunger* (1994), further solidified and defined the black metal style and sound, establishing Darkthrone as one of the early standard-bearers of black metal. In the following decades, the musical duo of Ted "Nocturno Culto" Skjellum (vocals, guitars, bass) and Gylve "Fenriz" Nagell (drums, additional guitar, bass) have become elder statesmen of black metal, with a tireless dedication to the metal underground in spite of their prominence. In keeping with this ethos, Nocturno Culto and Fenriz have disdained many of the show business aspects of the music industry, even as black metal's popularity has grown by leaps and bounds. This dedication to the underground, along with musical output that changes and evolves according to their whims rather than the expectations of fans or record labels, has endeared them to black metal fans worldwide.

A Blaze in the Northern Sky was conceived largely out of Darkthrone's dissatisfaction with their first album, in spite of its generally positive reception, and their growing disillusionment with death metal overall. In 1991, the band had been hard at work on a sophomore death metal record called *Goatlord*, which was in many ways an even more ambitious and intricate album than their debut. The then-quartet, including guitarist Ivar "Zephyrous" Enger and bassist Dag Nilsen, had worked incredibly hard writing and rehearsing their ultimate death metal opus, but Ted, Gylve, and Ivar were growing increasingly unsatisfied and restless with the more technical material. They began to worry that they were painting themselves into a corner, and they had also been reveling in the "primitive" sound and uncomplicated musical aesthetic of older underground metal like Celtic Frost and Bathory. Between the three of them, they decided that this was the direction that Darkthrone should take as well. Dag Nilsen, for his part, was apparently none too pleased to abandon *Goatlord* but agreed to stay on and play the sessions.[1]

This decision left Darkthrone in a slightly problematic situation, as they were already booked to record at Creative Studios in Kolbotn in about five months. They hurriedly wrote three new songs in their new "primitive" black metal style— "Kathaarian Life Code," "Where Cold Winds Blow," and "In the Shadow of the Horns"—and set about reworking material from *Goatlord* into the remaining three songs. Of those three,

"Paragon Belial" and "The Pagan Winter" are patchworks of older death metal material and more "blackened" elements, while the song structure of "A Blaze in the Northern Sky" remains more or less intact from the version on *Goatlord*, but with a markedly different approach to the drum performance in some parts. The album's running order intermingles the older and newer material, opening with two of the new black metal tracks ("Kathaarian Life Code" and "In the Shadow of the Horns"), switching gears to the older "Paragon Belial," returning to black metal with "Where Cold Winds Blow," and then closing with "A Blaze in the Northern Sky" and "The Pagan Winter." Taken as a whole, the album is, then, a bit of a mixed affair stylistically, although the deliberately low-fi production does a lot to hold it all together. Although Peaceville Records had understandable reservations about the record, it was released in February 1992 for an international black metal audience that, it should be said, did not actually exist at the time. Yet, the album quickly came to have a profound influence on many metal musicians thanks to Peaceville's reach as a label and the fact that *Soulside Journey* had already established Darkthrone's status both in Norway and abroad.

As the first Norwegian black metal record to gain significant international distribution and attention, Darkthrone's *A Blaze in the Northern Sky* also marks the start of a broader turning point in the history of Scandinavian rock music. Prior to the advent of Norwegian black metal, most people in the English-speaking world would have been hard-pressed to name a distinctly Norwegian style of music, or any Norwegian singers or musicians. Even today, most English-speaking listeners' experience of Norwegian popular music would probably consist of "Take on Me," "What Does the Fox Say?," and the numerous hit songs written and/or produced by the Trondheim duo Stargate for pop stars like Rihanna and Beyoncé. The vast majority of those listeners also likely have no idea that those songs were written or performed by Norwegians. By nearly any measure, black metal seems to be the first self-consciously "Norwegian" music since the days of Edvard Grieg to reach a large audience beyond Scandinavia.

Because of this, black metal's Norwegianness has formed a central ingredient of its appeal for the global audience from the very beginning, and in some cases black metal might be these listeners' lone experience with Scandinavian culture. The intense sounds and images of Norwegian black metal were also undoubtedly underscored by the serious crimes perpetrated by some members of the Norwegian black metal scene in the early 1990s. As I imagine most people reading this book are well aware, a number of Norwegian black metal musicians and fans, led mostly by Varg Vikernes of Burzum and Øystein "Euronymous" Aarseth of Mayhem, embarked on a spree of arson attacks against Norwegian churches. These actions worked (as intended) to raise the profile of the scene significantly, both within the international metal underground and eventually in mainstream newspapers. In addition to sparking a tabloid furor, these crimes also served notice to the metal underground: here were bands who were serious enough about their anti-Christian views to essentially commit acts of terrorism. Relations between Vikernes and Aarseth progressively soured until the situation turned deadly, with Vikernes ultimately stabbing Aarseth to death at his apartment in Oslo in August 1993. In the ensuing investigation, it was also discovered that in August 1992 the drummer Bård "Faust" Eithun of Emperor had murdered Magne Andreasson, a gay man who had propositioned him in a park. This extreme criminal aspect of the scene propelled it into the global spotlight and remains one of the cornerstones of its notoriety, even though similar crimes have been vanishingly rare among black metallers worldwide. Many black metal musicians are likely quite relieved to leave those events in the past. This violent origin story also serves to maintain Norway as the crucible of black metal's formation as a coherent genre, an association that, however unfortunate, has ultimately proved rather lucrative.

In promoting their Norwegianness, these black metal musicians also took advantage of some lasting perceptions about Norway and Scandinavian/Arctic regions in the popular global imagination. Even though Norway's oil wealth has resulted in incredible prosperity and modernization since the latter half of the twentieth century, many non-Scandinavians imagine it as a quaint provincial area, if not a full-on wilderness. In that vein, Norwegian tourism is driven largely by the country's spectacular natural landscapes, while stories of legendary Vikings and mythical trolls continue to fascinate people around the world. For the rest of the world, the North continues to be imagined as a wild place of magic and danger, and black metal's primitivist musical aesthetic and violent past fit into that ideal neatly. Further, Norwegian black metal's preoccupation with Norse legends and wilderness effectively allowed it to continue building its reputation on these foundations long after the criminal element had been dealt with.

Recently, cultural scholars have begun exploring how these long-lingering ideas have cultivated an exoticized image of Scandinavian and Arctic peoples and cultures. In exploring such exoticism, Edward Saïd's concept of "orientalism" is a regular touchstone, referring to the patronizing, mystical, and often sexualized way that European art and literature has tended to depict Asian, Middle-Eastern, and African cultures.[2] For

Europeans, these perceptions informed the ways that people in continental Europe defined themselves in opposition to other cultures, but the concept also applies to those that are basically next door, including Eastern Europe and the Nordic regions. The Nordic variation on orientalism has been termed "borealism," and although borealism continues the condescending tone implicit in other forms of exoticism, it also highlights landscapes and mythologies in unique ways. In exploring *A Blaze in the Northern Sky*, I will be returning to borealism repeatedly, as I think it illuminates many of the things that have helped to make Norwegian black metal a global phenomenon. Notions of primitiveness, savagery, forbidding wilderness, and isolation are threaded through black metal music and discourse, even that produced in other parts of the world.

These associations have also rendered many of the sonic conventions of Norwegian black metal into almost a musical shorthand for Northernness. Even just a cursory glance through black metal record reviews and promotional materials finds numerous references to the music sounding "cold," "frozen," "misty," and so forth. These environmental associations can be quite serious or they can take on a more playful mode as an inside joke among black metal fans ("Oh man, that riff is so frosty!"). For their part, Norwegian black metal musicians have actively cultivated this connection between their music's idiosyncratic sonic qualities and the geographies of Scandinavia through their lyrics, album artwork, music videos, costuming, and merchandise. Given that musical perceptions often rely heavily on metaphors, particularly for non-musicians, it makes sense that the lyrical, visual, and ideological conceits of Norwegian black metal managed to imprint themselves on the musical sound. After all, a sound can't be "cold" in any literal sense, yet the eccentric lo-fi sonic aesthetics of Darkthrone and others in their circle were able to go from sounding "harsh," "weird," or just "bad," to evoking wintry landscapes and freezing winds. When this music is combined with the aura of violence and ancient paganism surrounding the Norwegian scene, it can draw forth an almost otherwordly atmosphere of ominous mystery.

Finally, Darkthrone's lengthy career also provides an opportunity to explore the twenty-first-century extreme metal scene's turn to nostalgia, manifesting in trends of classic album sets at festivals, revivals of older styles of metal by young metalheads, and in the unearthing of long-neglected bands. For Darkthrone, though, this isn't something new. In many respects, they have been motivated by metal nostalgia ever since *A Blaze in the Northern Sky* mined the sonic terrains of the 1980s metal underground in opposition to the ever-slicker productions of 1990s death metal. Since the mid-2000s, however, Darkthrone has moved away from their black metal style somewhat, instead writing music that indulges their love for 1980s hardcore punk and speed metal. Fenriz has also become something of a public evangelist for obscure metal bands from the past. The fact that this nostalgia emerged at a time when extreme metal has become much more popular and profitable is no coincidence. Within all of it, Darkthrone have retained a stalwart presence as elders of a local scene that continues to inspire musicians and fans around the world.

"Hear a Haunting Chant ..."

Writers on art and culture often tend to assume that they are writing about and for people who are very much like themselves. As an academic whose career involves writing about metal, I have realized that this is a dubious assumption to make. With this in mind, I hope it will not be too indulgent to include a little bit of my background with black metal as a fan and musician, and reflect a little on the issues I have encountered while approaching this music I deeply love from an academic viewpoint.

My introduction to extreme metal was via the Finnish death metal band Amorphis's *Land of Thousand Lakes* album, followed by albums by Samael, My Dying Bride, and Tiamat. As with many "first encounter" stories of metal, it was mostly coincidence: a matter of stumbling onto the person who happened to have these CDs in suburban Oklahoma in the mid-1990s. Beyond my dubbed copies of these albums, though, I was mostly unaware of black metal and the rest of the international metal scene. However, this changed in 1996 when *Spin* magazine published a lurid feature on the Norwegian black metal scene and the murders, suicides, allegations of cannibalism, and church burnings that had made it infamous.[3] The article had little to say about the music itself and focused mostly on the crimes and the participants' socially Darwinistic worldviews, punctuated with references to pagan magic and Anne-Rice-style vampirism. As a high-school student in the middle of the Bible Belt, there was something incredibly compelling and even a little frightening about it all, an almost palpable aura of genuine evil. Popular angst-ridden gothic/industrial rockers like Type O Negative and Nine Inch Nails seemed trite by comparison. I even recall my church's youth pastor referencing that *Spin* article at one point. However, it was several years before I heard any of the music, which was how it worked in the days before the Internet was widely available. Over the years, I have found this music and its fan culture to be sources of camaraderie, comfort, and (dare I say it) fun. I also eventually managed to begin exploring black metal as a personal creative and artistic endeavor, both within bands and on my own.

A long time passed before I gave much thought to the Norwegian context of this music. In some respects, I know I imagined some sort of innate cultural affinity with this music, given that my paternal grandfather's side of the family was from Norway. My thinking in this manner was probably a lot like other white Americans who list off the various European roots of their ancestors as if it reveals something essential about their individual character. However, back then I don't remember having much knowledge of Norway beyond black metal, some stuff about Vikings, and a cursory knowledge of Norse mythology. I eventually traveled to Oslo for a weekend in the early 2000s while visiting a couple of friends in the UK, and like many non-Scandinavian black metal fans, I was rather underwhelmed by its near-total lack of grimness. Even though black metal and Norway seem inseparable in the minds of metalheads around the world, it's clear that most Norwegians don't particularly enjoy listening to it, if they even know it exists in the first place.

Years later, black metal remains a significant part of my life in various ways. Music subcultures may normally be associated with disaffected youth, but there are of course by now plenty of other middle-aged black metal fans like me who have regular jobs, children, mortgages, and varying levels of residual disaffection. Yet, in spite of my long association with black metal, I should acknowledge the limits of my experiences with it. Although I have recorded and performed black metal music for years, I've never done extensive touring, promotions, or related activities. As an American, I obviously also don't have the direct cultural knowledge of someone who grew up in Norway or Scandinavia, which honestly caused me some anxiety about writing this book. I further appreciate that for many people black metal music expresses ritual and spiritual meanings that I cannot access as a non-practitioner. My perspectives on black metal also necessarily differ from black metallers who are women, queer-identified, and/or persons of color, many of whom find black metal's music and subculture simultaneously empowering and infuriating.

The fact that I am an academic musicologist who has researched black metal for the past fifteen years also certainly colors my views on the style and its subcultures. I imagine a number of readers are as surprised as I was to discover that an academic career can involve the study of black metal. Nevertheless, there is a growing body of cross-disciplinary scholarship on metal, including a learned society (*The International Society for Metal Music Studies*), a peer-reviewed journal (*Metal Music Studies*), and international academic conferences. Black metal has even inspired an esoteric philosophical branch called Black Metal Theory, whose symposia and publications often manage to be incredibly insightful while simultaneously remaining rather impenetrable, much like black metal itself. From the other side, writing academic research on black metal is also complicated somewhat by my life as a black metal fan, if only because academic discourse resists the sort of overt advocacy and hagiography that usually motivates fan writing. Academic researchers who study music and other artistic and cultural practices perhaps all face some version of this dilemma, in that we normally study things that we also enjoy as fans, participants, and consumers. On some level, the very existence of academic scholarship on a particular topic advocates implicitly for its cultural legitimacy, since, like it or not, university professors continue to embody a certain institutional and social authority. As a result, I imagine the idea of tweedy academics like myself analyzing black metal from my perch within a university music department also might engender some understandable hostility among some readers. I like to hope that my participation in black metal as a fan and musician gives me an insider perspective on some points, but I have definitely come to realize that the experiences of the academic metalhead are not those of most black metal fans and musicians, and vice versa. Indeed, I am steeped in academic cultural positions and values that make it difficult for me to appreciate black metal as "just music" or even to draw a line between work and leisure regarding it. Hence this book.

"Darkthrone Is Not a Political Band ..."

Yet, even as black metal music has been a source of deep artistic satisfaction and fellowship over the years, aspects of black metal's milieu remain troubling to me. Metalheads are often loath to air our scene's dirty laundry, if we even admit that it exists in the first place, and we get defensive when someone points it out. Given metal's long history of being disdained as a musical style and scapegoated as a vector of delinquency and social decay, this protective stance makes some sense. But rose-colored glasses mask some red flags. Metal fans and scholars often portray the various communities around this music as being peaceful and inclusive, but metal spaces (real and virtual) often remain subtly or overtly unwelcoming to women, persons of color, and queer-identified participants. Further, when these people tell their stories they are usually met with silence at best, but also often with open hostility, harassment, and personal threats. I am grateful for their courage in this regard, because my ability to reference their experiences in the first place is dependent on their willingness to take those risks.[4] Although black metal is a global phenomenon with dedicated participants across the globe, its geographic reach does not mean entrenched social inequalities are absent within metal scenes. In many (if not most) cases, they can be amplified. In Norway, black metal's nationalistic bent is often framed in terms of local countercultural resistance towards, variously, hegemonic Christianity, globalization, the collectivist ethos of Nordic social democracies, and/or the European Union, but it is also an intensification of beliefs about cultural identity and immigration long held by many Norwegians who would otherwise want nothing to do with black metal.[5] The masculinist and homophobic aspects of black metal subcultures likewise mirror those of wider society, suggesting that black metal's veneer of countercultural resistance is often simply reactionary and mostly serves to buttress existing social hierarchies.

In particular, the specters of racism and radical white nationalism haunt any discussion of black metal and its depictions of "Northernness." Although I don't want to overstate the influence of these associations, it would be dishonest to pretend they haven't affected the genre's music and listenership in some profound ways. It is clear that black metal scenes can provide fertile ground for expressions of ethnocentrism and xenophobic racism, and white nationalist organizations have employed black metal's countercultural stance as an entryway for recruitment. Further, black metal's love of provocation provides cover and deniability by obscuring boundaries between subcultural and political expressions, and between public performance and private belief. Even bands who are connected to violent white nationalist organizations rarely sing about such things directly, preferring instead standard black metal themes of nature, mythology, esoteric spiritualities, and references to local heritage. For certain factions within the genre's wider subculture, these black metal tropes can be understood within a thinly coded ethno-nationalist context, and this aspect lets the music continue to act as a stealth recruiting tool.

This situation can make researching black metal a bit of an ethical and moral minefield. Benjamin Teitelbaum's research on white nationalist groups in Sweden provides an insightful look into this dilemma.[6] In particular, he notes that one of the prime directives of ethnographic and anthropological research is solidarity between researcher and subject. In the end, any knowledge gained from the research depends on it, because few people would interact honestly with an academic researcher whom they didn't trust, and earning trust through deception or with ill intent generally runs counter to accepted research ethics. The central dilemma is whether the insights gained about oppressive, privileged, and even violent groups are worth the moral compromises that are necessary to acquire that knowledge. Perhaps foremost is the question of whether the research could potentially be used by those groups to advance and legitimize their agendas.

My perspective on this side of black metal is also informed by my involvement in the black metal scene in Colorado and Utah. Over the years, I have seen on occasion how neo-Nazis and white nationalists can thrive and even become prominent within regional metal scenes, shaping the tone and makeup of the scene in numerous ways both obvious and subtle. To a certain extent, it seems that participating in black metal has often required either willfully ignoring the existence of this contingent or tacitly accepting their participation. Additionally, these people don't always clearly identify themselves or their ties to such movements, and they may be otherwise dependable and solid members of the scene. Yet, also, painting with too broad a brush could easily tarnish musicians and other participants who have never been connected with extremist political movements, or who have since cut ties with those ideologies. The situation also cultivates a certain paranoia, and there is sometimes even a suspicion that bands who take pains to claim political neutrality may be winking when they do so, as if they doth protest too much. I am also deeply aware that I am writing in the aftermath of the 2011 terrorist attacks in Norway and the ascendance of the far-right in Europe and the USA over the last few years. Things that could potentially have been waved away as simple provocation less than a decade ago take on additional significance in such an environment.

Darkthrone themselves haven't been immune. The artwork for their 1994 album *Transilvanian Hunger* infamously included the inscription "Norsk Arisk Black Metal" (Norwegian Aryan Black Metal) on its back cover, and in the press release for the album stated that any critics should be "thoroughly patronized for [their] obviously Jewish behavior." Their record label distanced themselves from those statements and eventually elicited a formal apology in which Fenriz explained that Norwegian youth used "Arisk" as an assertion of authenticity meaning "true" or "pure" and that "Jewish" was slang for "idiotic." Having grown up in and around the Southern

USA, I actually have little trouble believing that casually racist and anti-Semitic terms might've been a regular part of Scandinavian youth slang in the 1990s, but even if it works as an explanation it doesn't actually defuse the statement. Nor really did their statement in the insert of their following album, which they named *Panzerfaust* after a German anti-tank weapon: "Darkthrone is certainly not a Nazi band nor a political band. Those of you who still might think so, you can lick Mother Mary's asshole in eternity." In more recent years, however, Fenriz has repeatedly repudiated the statements and expressed regret about making them, and as far as I can tell he seems sincere in his contrition.

In the documentary *Once Upon a Time in Norway*, Nocturno Culto muses at one point that things would have been easier if they'd just kept to death metal because then it was only about the music; playing death metal didn't require believing in any particular ideology.[7] Even though it may be impossible to escape from the shadow of black metal's flirtations with violence and neofascism, and those aspects shouldn't be discounted or ignored, my hope is to highlight aspects of the music and its legacy that have often been overshadowed by the crimes in its past and by some black metallers' affinity for political extremism and provocation. As a result, the fact that this book's agenda focuses mostly on black metal's musical style and its life as a Norwegian cultural export requires a moral compromise on my part in that the nastier aspects of black metal subcultures may not get the thorough airing-out that they deserve. Hopefully, any insights gained from my focus on musical style and production wind up being worth that cost. There is room for optimism, however, as some black metal musicians and communities are pursuing a vision of black metal that is deliberately more inclusive and that seeks to decouple black metalness from right-wing extremism. While such reclamation takes a lot of time and effort, it is encouraging that some black metal fans are forging a path that maintains black metal's countercultural ethos without giving in to bigotry and chauvinism. The past shouldn't be forgotten, but neither should it determine the genre's future.

With these caveats in mind, it's time to go back to Norway in the early 1990s, when all of this got started. The book starts out with an exploration of black metal's history, and its evolution from an ill-defined musical aesthetic to a major commercial force in the global metal music industry. The next chapter, "Where Cold Winds Blow," examines how the borealistic preconceptions about Norway and the North worked to inform and direct black metal's musical life as an internationally recognized genre of distinctly Norwegian music, particularly for the hordes of fans (like me) who are not from Scandinavia. The third chapter digs into black metal as a musical style and production aesthetic, highlighting the ways that *A Blaze in the Northern Sky* presages many of black metal's distinctive musical idioms while keeping one foot in the death metal style that Darkthrone began with. The final chapter checks in with Darkthrone in 2020, exploring how their stylistic shifts reflect changes in metal culture and music consumption in the years since *A Blaze in the Northern Sky* was released.

1 "In the Shadow of the Horns"

Face of the Goat in the Mirror
Eyes Burn like (an) October Sunrise
As Once they Gazed upon the Hillside
Searching for the Memories …
In the Shadow of the Horns

Like all histories, musical histories are fraught territory under the best of circumstances, and to say that Norwegian black metal's situation is more burdened than most would be an understatement. Untangling music history's usual mix of strategic omissions, exaggerations, score-settling, and bald-faced lies is difficult enough without adding in suicides, arsons, Satanism, and murder. Yet, black metal fans and musicians obviously have a lot at stake in how the story of the genre is told, and by whom, as do the record labels, tour promoters, festival organizers, magazines, and venues that currently manage the business of black metal. Such histories establish the boundaries of the genre and impose organization within those imagined borders, thus working to channel the genre's present and future activities. Choosing what to emphasize, what to intentionally ignore, and what to conveniently forget then becomes paramount, because those choices can create their own kind of inertia. Small wonder then that the development and history of black metal, and what aspects of its past should matter to black metallers in the twenty-first century, has already generated so much ink, both from those who lived through it and people like me who came to the scene later.

As such, this chapter is going to engage in a little bit of historiography and explore how black metal's history has been written and Darkthrone's place within it. There are two main threads to follow. The first thread traces aspects of musical and visual style, particularly how Darkthrone's black metal aesthetic on *A Blaze in the Northern Sky* mined older metal and hardcore punk styles for inspiration, and how that aesthetic then blossomed further. The second thread explores how black metal's sensationalistic coverage in the media aligns with other late twentieth-century moral panics around rock music and violence, fueling the notoriety that helped to popularize Norwegian black metal worldwide. These two threads ultimately intertwine, however, because the intervening decades have seen black metal's diffusion into "regular" society, as has happened with numerous other deviant or countercultural musical subcultures over the years. Naturally, this process also sparks moments of cognitive dissonance and a bit of a perpetual identity crisis, as both the subculture and wider society work to reconcile themselves to the new situation.

"… And Now the Black Metal!"

Writers on black metal typically divide the genre's stylistic musical arc into three "waves": an initial birth in the 1980s, development into a coherent genre in the early 1990s, and a third wave beginning in the late 1990s which is marked by increasing diversity and popularity. As with all stylistic histories, the boundaries between these periods are a bit nebulous, and such a conception is not without its problems, but it gives a general idea of black metal's trajectory from an ill-defined style of underground metal to an essential cog in the international metal music industries. Although Norway is where black metal found its first expression as a coherent musical genre, the musical style hearkens back to the mid-1980s, drawing particular inspiration from the British band Venom, the Swiss bands Hellhammer and Celtic Frost, the Swedish band Bathory, and the Danish band Mercyful Fate. Celtic Frost, Hellhammer, and Bathory provided much of the sonic blueprint, as their music featured harsh guitar timbres, low-budget recording aesthetics, punk-influenced fast tempos, and occult lyrics. Venom provided the subgenre with its moniker in their song "Black Metal" from the album of the same name. Venom also cultivated a campy evil image that Norwegian musicians sought to expand upon, looking to move beyond Venom's cartoonish theatrics into something more authentic. Mercyful Fate is included in histories of black metal largely due to the influence of their singer, King Diamond, whose black and white makeup, occult-focused lyrics, and apparent dedication to seriously practicing Satanism were an inspiration for many later black metallers. It should be emphasized, though, that this first wave of black metal was defined retroactively by black metallers in the 1990s as a way to create a lineage for themselves. It does not represent a distinct musical style, nor did any of those bands in the 1980s refer to themselves as a "black metal" band, even though it is now commonplace to group them together under that banner.[1] In addition, none of these bands from the 1980s displayed the enduring fascination with nature and Nordic landscapes that became a defining characteristic of Norwegian black metal. But, to borrow a quote from Vladimir Nabokov, "That which does not have a name does not exist."[2]

In the late 1980s and early 1990s, a coterie of Norwegian metal bands, often referred to as "The Black Circle," began developing black metal into a coherent and self-identifying aesthetic, motivated by their opposition to the growing commercialization and standardization of death metal. This "second wave" of black metal included many of the bands that came to define the genre, including Mayhem, Burzum, Emperor, Enslaved, Immortal, Ulver, and Darkthrone. Many of these bands cultivated a dramatic musical style, at times employing complex harmonies, folk-ish melodies, and using keyboards to lend their songs a touch of the epic and fantastic. However, compared to their compatriots, Darkthrone have always been more musically conservative in their approach, favoring the punkish simplicity of 1980s black metal rather than the sweeping quasi-orchestral grandeur of bands like Emperor and Enslaved. Even from the beginning, Darkthrone have been representative of the nostalgic and purist aspect of black metal, often preferring long-established aesthetic boundaries to their peers' more progressive tendencies. This tension between fidelity to older ideals and musical exploration became an important aspect of black metal's existence as a coherent and self-identifying musical aesthetic.

The middle section of "In the Shadow of the Horns" provides an illustrative example of Darkthrone's revivalist ideal and how it drives their conception of black metal. The song is primarily a mid-paced affair up until around four minutes into the song when the music pauses briefly, and Fenriz then begins playing a fast beat at around 145 bpm. This is followed by an exhortation, "and now the black metal!," and a new guitar riff. The first half of the riff creates a hemiola effect by playing a slower triplet rhythm over the faster drums, while the second half is in a tremolo-picked sixteenth note rhythm. Taken together, the guitar riff and the particular drum pattern are evocative of hardcore punk of the 1980s, particularly the English band Discharge. The example below compares this riff from "In the Shadow of the Horns" to Discharge's "The Final Blood Bath" (1982)

In particular, the drum pattern of the two is basically identical, although Fenriz adds progressively more double-kick drum as this section continues, which makes it sound more "metal." For hardcore punk fans, this drum pattern became so closely identified with Discharge (and their numerous musical progeny) that it was eventually named the "D-beat" in their honor. Yet, when Darkthrone proclaim "and now the black metal!" they might also be referring specifically to Venom's

Example 1.1 *Darkthrone, "In the Shadow of the Horns."*

Example 1.2 *Discharge, "The Final Bloodbath."*

Example 1.3 *Venom, "Black Metal."*

1982 song "Black Metal." The main verse riff of "Black Metal" is likewise played over a D-beat drum pattern and features a triplet turnaround at the end for a hemiola effect akin to that from "In the Shadow of the Horns."

It is important to note, though, that even if Darkthrone intentionally meant to reference Venom's "Black Metal" in this section (and I don't know if they did), the characteristics of these riffs and drum patterns were shared across numerous metal and punk bands in the 1980s. Bathory, in particular, was also obviously taking many cues from hardcore punk in their early albums. There's also something very Motörhead-ish going on; after all, these examples are all only a few degrees of separation from "Ace of Spades." In the liner notes for the Darkthrone boxed set *Black Death and Beyond*, Fenriz even goes so far as to describe this section of the song as the "Motörhead d-beat part."[3] This revivalist ideal also illuminates the fact that in the 1980s many of the genre divisions between various flavors of heavy metal and punk had yet to be fully articulated in the first place, much less enforced. Darkthrone's invocation of this era creates a certain irony though, in that their concept of "black metal" as a genre relied on referencing a time period marked by a comparative lack of genre definitions. But perhaps "In the Shadow of the Horns" is just another example of the adage that sometimes one of the most productive ways to do something new is to do something old.

The early 1990s also saw the development of black metal's distinctive visual aesthetic, both in terms of artwork and performance. Black metal band logos are usually rather intricate and symmetrical hand-drawn affairs in which the band's name is stylized and obscured within a more complex design. Darkthrone's band logo, for instance, looks rather like a tangle of branches with moss. Of course, distinct typefaces, band logos, and mascots like Iron Maiden's "Eddie" had already been a hallmark of metal for decades, but the almost manneristic approach adopted by black metal and other extreme metal styles demonstrates an impulse towards obscurity. They function almost like occult sigils, confounding non-metalheads while communicating information to those who are in the know. With enough experience, even a completely illegible logo can convey a lot about a band's musical style to a knowledgeable fan. Norwegian black metal also popularized the use of black and white "corpsepaint," which usually features a ghostly white base with blacked-in eyes and various lines running from the eyes and mouth. In some cases, particular designs are tied so closely to one individual performer that they are essentially an underground version of the makeup worn by the members of KISS. In his extensive interviews with Norwegian black metal musicians, Dayal Patterson notes that many of them recall owning KISS trading cards as children.[4] These designs work essentially as masks which serve to render the black metal performers more-or-less anonymous, drawing a clear line between their black metal persona and their everyday life, a division that is further augmented by their regular use of stage names.[5] Black metal performers also often don gothic or medieval costumes, sometimes including weaponry. This concern for theatricality ultimately became one of the aspects that helped to distinguish black metal from death metal and thrash metal, neither of which saw the need to indulge in such performance conceits.

Yet, once black metal was given this sense of definition, many black metallers self-consciously pushed the boundaries of the style. In the latter half of the 1990s and into the twenty-first century, many bands in this "third wave" of black metal sought new inspirations and musical fusions. Bands like Thorns, Dodheimsgard, Ulver, and Peccatum began incorporating synthesized and sampled sounds from industrial and techno music. Although keyboards have long been a part of black metal's instrumentation, prior to this time they had been used primarily to emulate orchestras and choirs, and occasionally pianos and organs. The mid-1990s onward also saw increasing interest in combining black metal with various traditional and folk instruments, cultivating the style that came to be known as "folk metal." In the early twenty-first century, a number of bands began fusing the furious rhythmic drive of black metal with idioms from indie and "shoegaze" music, including chiming clean guitars, major-key chord progressions, and soaring vocal melodies. This style was epitomized by the French band Alcest, whose music occasionally resembles that of the new-age star Enya, but with metal drums and guitars. Bands like Aluk Todolo and Ved Buens Ende cultivated idiosyncratic musical aesthetics with roots in various avant-garde musics. Increasingly, for some bands, black metal became a stylistic selection within a wider palette of musical influences and options rather than a genre they would fully inhabit.

The first decades of the twenty-first century also saw the increasing commercialization of black metal, and extreme metal more generally. Bands like Dimmu Borgir adopted more normative aesthetics for both their sound and visuals, increasingly employing a more polished production that prized heaviness and clarity while leaving behind idiosyncratic hand-drawn logos in favor of clearer typefaces.[6] Meanwhile, the British black metal band Cradle of Filth achieved immense commercial success by cultivating a gothic vampire image drawn from Hammer horror films and Anne Rice novels, and writing lyrics laced with sadomasochistic eroticism and dry wit. Increased high-speed Internet access since the late 1990s also certainly played a role in metal's growing popularity as well, promoting metal fandom by providing access to extreme metal music and online communities.

Naturally, the growing popularity and stylistic diversity of black metal also prompted a nostalgic backlash favoring the rawer underground aesthetics of bands like Darkthrone. Given that Darkthrone's initial forays into black metal were themselves reactionary, the twenty-first-century variant could possibly be termed "neo-nostalgia," in that it is nostalgic for the nostalgias of the past. Academicizing aside, for many participants, the underground of black metal remains a site of countercultural resistance towards commercialization and mainstream society, both in terms of worldview and musical aesthetics. That it does this while simultaneously reaching fairly large audiences around the world seems deeply contradictory, but black metal is far from the first style of popular music to achieve the very popularity it disdains.

Satanic Panics

Norwegian black metal's transformation from an obscure music scene into an international subculture was ultimately catalyzed by some musicians who engaged in serious crimes in the early 1990s. In 1992, Varg Vikernes of the band Burzum embarked on a series of church arsons with several other black metal musicians, partly as a publicity stunt and partly as a symbolic retribution for the Christianizing of Norway about a thousand years ago. The criminal activity came to a head in 1993 when Vikernes murdered Øystein "Euronymous" Aarseth, the guitarist of Mayhem and another dominant persona in the scene. The ensuing investigation also revealed Bård "Faust" Eithun's guilt in the then-unsolved murder of Magne Andreasson. The ensuing trials and media attention sparked the rise of black metal's visibility on an international level, and since the late 1990s the story has inspired a number of books, documentaries, and a Hollywood film, *Lords of Chaos* (2019). For fans abroad, these crimes conjured up exoticized visions of violent pagan primitivism that became an essential ingredient to black metal's particular terroir. The details of these events have been well documented, so my concern here is mostly with the aftermath of these crimes and how they came to form the backbone of Norwegian black metal's existence as a commercial product, even as many musicians and fans look to move past them.

Contemporary media portrayals of the church burnings and violence in Norway focused primarily on the most prurient aspects of the Black Circle's crime spree, of which there was admittedly no shortage. Vikernes and Euronymous clearly reveled in the notoriety. In their March 1993 interview with the British metal magazine *Kerrang!* they claimed to be the organizers of a militant circle of Satanic Terrorists and remarked on the church burnings and their attempts to intimidate other metal bands. They were cagey about their involvement in the arsons, although they supported them. Euronymous discussed the 1991 shotgun suicide of Mayhem's singer Dead (Per

Ohlin) with remarkable callousness, noting that it was a great promotional tool for Mayhem and claiming that he had "no feelings left" and didn't care if people within his own circle died. He mentioned, but didn't verify, the rumors that he had taken photos of Dead's corpse (true) and that he had collected pieces of Dead's skull and given them to people he deemed worthy (also supposedly true). Vikernes, who was then using the Tolkein-inspired pseudonym Count Grishnackh, proclaimed that humans are worthless and stupid, expressed support for fascist dictatorships, and predicted that he would become the dictator of Scandinavia. He also stated that he was a Viking and that this meant he supported war and had no qualms about murder. *Kerrang!* also explicitly linked the Norwegian black metal scene with neo-Nazism.[7]

In hindsight, such nihilistic and grandstanding poses seem almost laughable in their desire to deliberately provoke and generate press coverage, but for the fact that these men did in fact commit arsons and one of them ultimately murdered the other. Following Euronymous's murder, *Kerrang!* and other metal magazines published interviews with Vikernes in which he dismissed Euronymous's death. In these features, the magazines also dutifully covered the impending releases of Mayhem's *De Mysteriis dom Sathanas* and Burzum's *Hvis Lyset Tar Oss,* providing yet another example of how untimely violent death provides an unparalleled kind of publicity. Add to this the fact that Varg Vikernes actually played session bass on *De Mysteriis dom Sathanas* (his tracks were supposed to have been re-recorded, but it seems that this was never done), and the album takes on the dubious distinction of likely being the only commercially available recording in which both a murderer and his victim are playing together.

However, it is important to take a step back and put the media coverage of the Norwegian scene into a broader context of depictions of heavy metal and Satanism in the 1980s and 1990s. The media narratives on the crimes in Norway echoed the American and British "Satanic panics" in the late 1980s. These series of panics conjured up an imaginary wave of child kidnappings, sexual abuse, and ritualized murders by hidden cabals of Satanists. Heavy metal and punk music, along with role-playing games like Dungeons and Dragons, were accused of encouraging (if not outright causing) Satanism, drug and alcohol use, violence, sex, and suicide among young listeners. Metalheads and punks were cast as "folk devils," a term first described in Stanley Cohen's *Folk Devil's and Moral Panics* (1972).[8] The folk devil is used as an all-purpose scapegoat for a variety of social problems, ultimately sparking a wider moral panic because of their supposed deviance. The 1980s were a time of significant social anxiety and dislocation, and trends of family disintegration, newly working mothers, and working-class economic stagnation created fertile ground for such a panic and sparked the need to create a folk devil figure of some sort. Accusations of Satanic subliminal messages and backmasking dogged Led Zeppelin, Judas Priest, and Ozzy Osbourne in the 1980s and 1990s, even resulting in lawsuits that sought to blame their music for the suicides of several young fans. In extreme cases, participation in heavy metal or punk subcultures was essentially pathologized as evidence of mental instability. The efforts of the Parent's Music Resource Center further mobilized parental concerns about heavy metal, now with a veneer of institutional neutrality, ultimately culminating in congressional hearings in 1985.[9]

Further events in the 1990s echoed this moral panic, particularly the 1994 conviction of three young metalheads in

West Memphis for the gruesome murders of three young boys. On evidence based mostly on the accused's metal fandom, the three earned one death sentence and two life sentences, which were ultimately appealed, resulting in their release in 2011. Although the case is officially closed, those responsible almost certainly escaped justice. The 1996 school shooting at Columbine High School in Colorado likewise sparked concerns that the perpetrators had been motivated by goth and industrial music and fashion. For several years after the massacre, goth culture and fashion were linked with violence in media programs and in some cases banned by school administrators. Norwegian black metal seemed to actualize these fears over metal music, in no small part because in this case the musicians in question actually committed serious crimes themselves rather than just supposedly influencing listeners' behavior through their lyrics and cover art. Further, there was no need to search for Satanic subtexts or subliminal messages; the occultism was all in plain sight and apparently done with utter seriousness.

Unsurprisingly, Norwegian black metal's sensationalistic past casts a long shadow over the scene and dominates narratives of the genre to this day. In particular, the first book-length history of Norwegian black metal, Michael Moynihan and Didrik Søderlind's 1998 book *Lords of Chaos: The Bloody Rise of the Satanic Metal Underground*, focuses on the church burnings and murders while digging up a few other obscure bands in Europe and the USA whose members committed similar crimes. As a way to tie these disparate characters together, it also indulges in a bit of Jungian esotericism, arguing that black metal represents an atavistic cultural revival with Varg Vikernes of Burzum acting as a sort of avatar of pre-Christian pagan European traditions.[10] Although there is undoubtedly a compelling thread between black metal's visual aesthetic and the masking and costuming practiced by pre-Christian groups in Europe and Scandinavia (and elsewhere), making this point does not require positing a metaphysical connection between the two.[11] And perhaps there is also an element of disappointment at work, in that some of the musicians who made such evocative and transporting music turned out to just be run-of-the-mill ethno-nationalists and authoritarians.[12] The book's promotion of this cultural fantasy ultimately served to amplify black metal's connections with far-right extremist movements, and also allowed the book to acquaint readers with those groups and probably even quietly double as a recruiting tool. The second edition of *Lords of Chaos* tempered some of these aspects, but part of the book's ultimate legacy has been to promote black metal as essentially tied to right-wing extremism and violence. However, it should be said that the book does possibly allow some of these Norwegian black metallers to show their true colors, as when Mayhem's drummer Hellhammer goes on record stating unreservedly that "black metal is for white people" and wishing that the church burners had targeted mosques instead, ideally with plenty of worshippers inside. Of course, the fact that such statements go unchallenged also leaves the reader to wonder if they arise from a sincere belief or just a desire to provoke and offend. For many years, however, *Lords of Chaos* was one of the only available English-language sources to treat black metal in-depth with semi-scholarly language, complete with plenty of interviews, and as such it has probably had an outsized effect on perceptions of the genre in the Anglophone world especially. Scholars like myself who write about black metal continue to grapple with the book's legacy, even as it remains a valuable primary source.

Thankfully, some subsequent histories and collections of interviews (notably Dayal Patterson's *Cult Never Dies* series) have filled in other perspectives on black metal, both in Norway and beyond. Many other documentaries and histories continue to focus on the criminal history of the Norwegian black metal scene, which admittedly makes some sense. After all, the histories of Burzum and Mayhem in particular make for tragic and compelling storytelling, with no shortage of intriguing and complex characters. It's almost impossible not to lead with the violence, even when discussing figures like Darkthrone who weren't directly involved in it. But focusing on that short period only conveys part of the story of Norwegian black metal; in my view some of the most interesting things happen after the criminals have been removed from the scene and those who are left have to figure out what to do now.

Incorporation and Recuperation

Lords of Chaos and similar histories sometimes read as an attempt to preserve the "folk devil" status of black metallers as genuine threats to the existing social order, which highlights the fact that moral panics are temporary phenomena. Indeed, one of the main limitations of books like *Lords of Chaos* is that they confine black metal's origin and authentic existence solely to its brief period of actual mayhem, along with its alliance with various religious and political ideologies, rather than allowing for further aesthetic development.[13] In Cohen's sociological model of folk devils, once a threat is identified it is then stereotyped and stylized by the media, while institutions and other social guardians pronounce solutions and ways of coping with it. Eventually, however, the conditions or circumstances that sparked the moral panic evolve, the media moves on and the offending group becomes less of a target. But rather than fade into the background as the media cycle winds down, like targets of many earlier moral panics, black metal instead ultimately became a more visible part of the Norwegian entertainment industry.

This situation highlights the fact that even after the crest of a moral panic, the nonconformist stance of the subculture in question often remains ripe for commercialization. Dick Hebdige's 1979 book *Subculture: The Meaning of Style* provides a productive framework for illuminating Norwegian black metal's evolution from an obscure underground phenomenon to a pillar of the international metal music industry and an "official" Norwegian cultural product.[14] Hebdige's work is focused on British youth culture after World War II, particularly the class-consciousness of punk, and he is concerned mostly with style and fashion rather than musical idioms. However, the trajectory he traces for punk's life as a form of counter-cultural youth resistance finds many parallels in the popularization of black metal. Both punk and black metal initially provoked shock and horror along with morbid fascination. In both cases, the tabloid press quickly amplified and sensationalized the subculture's social deviance, portraying them as irredeemable outcasts. However, this sensationalism and marginalization does not last forever. Hebdige argues that in the end the subculture in question is ultimately both diffused and defused, its members and symbols reclaimed by "respectable" society, with any social ruptures repaired. He refers to this process as "incorporation."

Hebdige breaks his process of incorporation down further into "commodity" forms and "ideological" forms to more closely trace how subcultural styles and ideas become incorporated into wider popular culture. Black metal provides an instructive example of the ways that subcultural symbols, fashions, and musical styles can be converted into mass-produced objects for wider consumption. After all, participation in metal subcultures, and rock music more generally, has long been a leisure activity that concerns itself primarily with consumption and collecting. Attending concerts and gathering massive (and expensive) collections of recordings, shirts, patches, and other memorabilia remains an important indicator of one's dedication to the scene and a marker of status. As with other sorts of collecting, the rarer the items, the better.

Since the idea of consumption is already valued within metal subcultures, the next step is to commodify black metal's various musical, sonic, and visual idioms. As Hebdige put it, although these subcultural styles might start their lives by issuing symbolic challenges, they end by establishing new sets of conventions and creating new commodities.[15] For example, the raw "lo-fi" sound of Darkthrone's early black metal records would have seemed amateurish by the standards of even most underground metal at the time. But even something marked by supposed incompetence can become commodified, codified, and "frozen" (in every sense of the word) as a marker of style and subcultural affinity. The "artisanal" subcultural aesthetic, in this case a cheap-sounding and idiosyncratic production, becomes a criterion for the genre instead of representing any sort of resistance to popularization. Once something like this is understood as a norm, it also becomes more comprehensible to the wider public as a sonic symbol of black metal-ness instead of just sowing revulsion or confusion.

Perhaps even more so than the music, the fashion and visual aesthetics of subcultures like black metal are also ripe for commodification, although perhaps not to the extent that was experienced by the punk and goth subcultures in the 1970s and 1980s. The black metal fashion aesthetic aligned rather well with pre-existing metal and goth fashions, allowing black metal shirts to easily find their way into specialty stores and suburban mall chains like Hot Topic (which certainly deserves a lot of credit, or perhaps blame, for popularizing gothic and "alternative" fashions across the USA in the 1990s–2000s). Makers of medieval garb like chain mail, spiked arm bracers, and costume weaponry were also assuredly glad to find a new market for their products beyond professional costume designers and medieval reenactors. The visual appearance of black metal logos, which often seem impenetrable to outsiders, is also a clearly defined aesthetic that can be easily borrowed, remixed, and parodied. In the end, the visual markers that identify black metal as an oppositional underground counterculture end up functioning like any other sort of brand identity.

The ultimate end of this commodity form, according to Hebdige, is an ideological form of recuperation in which the subculture's members and its stylistic aesthetics are reclaimed by mainstream society.[16] The subculture's deviance, once a source of dread and fascination, becomes minimized as the subculture's participants are increasingly portrayed as regular folks with regular lives who admittedly have some peculiar musical tastes and hobbies. In the case of Norwegian black metal, the incarceration and rehabilitation of its criminal cohort allowed the genre's history of violence to become the stuff of myth rather than a present danger to society. Satanic symbols and occult or violent imagery became show business spectacles again, perhaps even for those who express such beliefs sincerely. The efforts of the Norwegian media industries and cultural institutions to promote black metal as an official cultural product is another one of the endgames of this process. So too perhaps are books like this one, which depend on black metal having gained some measure of aesthetic merit deemed worthy of investigating at length.

In Hebdige's model, the moment a subculture comes to the attention of wider society is the moment it begins to decline from resistance into commodification and commercialism. But this framing is maybe a little too cut-and-dried for our purposes, especially since the relationship between the "true" black metal subculture and the media industries has been fairly ambiguous from the very beginning. After all, the church arsons of the 1990s were conceived by Varg Vikernes, at least in part, as a publicity stunt to promote Burzum albums. Making class-based resistance the heart of subculture also has its limitations. After all, many social groups based around music may not see this sort of cultural or political resistance as a primary goal or even a part of their practices. Metal is notably difficult to pin down in this regard, due to many participants' long-standing ambivalence toward overt politicization, regardless of their personal views. Further, people involved in a particular musical subculture often drift in and out of active or visible participation or migrate between various separate subcultures that may or may not overlap. Beyond music subcultures, the importance of consumption and collecting to cult media fandoms of all types (science fiction, comic books, *Star Trek*, etc.) also raises the possibility that the academic emphasis on "resistance" might mostly be a tactic intended to obscure the stain of consumerism from fan practices and thereby assert their legitimacy as objects of study.[17] As a result of these limitations, subcultural studies in the decades since Hebdige's *Subculture* have articulated a number of subtler models to account for this diversity in experience, including "neo-tribes," "art worlds," and the more holistic "scene," which encompasses not just fans and musicians but also related networks of promotion, performance, and distribution.[18] With this in mind, it is perhaps also worth questioning the overriding pessimism and fatalism that animates Hebdige's model. Although it might be anathema to say so within both subcultural studies and underground music subcultures, the fact that oppositional subcultures almost inevitably become part of the fabric of mainstream society may not necessarily lead to degradation or dilution. It certainly leads to change, but viewing that change as inherently negative mostly illustrates one's personal politics rather than conveying something intrinsic to the music. Suffice to say, the "us vs. them" model of Hebdige's class-conscious subcultures is ultimately too simplistic, even if the overall trajectory seems to hold up in the case of black metal's entry into more visible and profitable levels of the entertainment industry.

The narrative of inevitable assimilation into the mainstream also hides a significant problem in plain sight. Although black metallers, punks, goths, and other subcultural participants regularly draw a clear line between their musical subculture and the mainstream, the "mainstream" is often so ill-defined that is almost chimerical. Thus, the point at which subculture stops and mainstream begins is rendered as an ever-moving and amorphous boundary. But as vague as these distinctions may be, they obviously remain incredibly important both for subcultural insiders and outsiders, and, indeed, the very existence of subcultural studies hinges on a tacit acceptance that these divisions exist and are meaningful. The academic discourse in subcultural studies has also sometimes seemed to function as a reaction against the very subcultures in question, an attempt to hold their difference accountable to expert knowledge.[19] For black metallers, collecting records, wearing metal shirts, and participating in the scene remains a personal statement of belonging to a group that has not been fully assimilated. The distinctions are also important for those outside the subculture who might, rightly or wrongly, identify its participants as a problem that needs solving.

(In)authenticities

Predictably, black metal's inclusion in more commercialized and socially respectable arenas, "mainstream" or not, has also put its fan culture and its musicians into a state of nearly perpetual crisis concerning authenticity and sincerity. It is far from alone in this regard. Rock music more generally has been dealing with this authenticity paradox since the 1960s, when rock music became associated with youth rebellion, individuality, protest, and rejection of mass "pop" culture while simultaneously becoming massively popular. As several scholars have noted, rock music's concepts of authenticity are rooted in a certain strain of Romanticism, particularly in its reaction against the conformity of modern society.[20] Rock music looked for this nonconformity in various and even contradictory places. The 1950s and 1960s saw a number of American musicians and audiences looking to the musical traditions of marginalized racial and economic groups, largely African-American blues music and rural white "folk" music. Meanwhile, many English rock musicians of the 1960s and 1970s looked to the avant-garde, especially the many art-school graduates (John Lennon, Syd Barrett, Brian Eno) within the psychedelic and progressive rock scenes. Yet these approaches and others all ultimately wind up framing rock authenticity as tied to individual creativity and personal expression conceived in opposition to conformist society.[21] In many ways, this ideal is an echo of eighteenth- and nineteenth-century Romanticism, which often conceived of the creative individual as being outside and even above "normal" society. The artist's personal journey into him or herself is paramount, and the artist's works are taken to be sincere expressions of that journey.

Yet, of course there is more to it, simply because of the numerous contradictions at work. For example, although rock generally prizes individuality and nonconformity, many genres (including metal) also value community and continuity with existing older traditions. In order to deal with these complexities, the musicologist Keir Keightley has articulated a useful model for rock authenticity that follows two threads of authenticity: one tied to Romantic ideology and one tied to Modernism.[22] Broadly, Romanticism locates authenticity in the past, seeking refuge from the confusions of modernity in nature and idealized traditional rural communities. Modernism, on the other hand, seeks to break ties with the past and escape the current situation via experimentation, innovation, and radical change. In Keightley's formulation, Romantic authenticity manifests in genres that value tradition and musical "roots," a sense of community, emotional sincerity, belief in a core essential sound, and a love of "live" natural sounds. Modernist authenticity, on the other hand, promotes experimentation and fusions, individualism, irony and sarcasm, and often highlights the use of technology.[23] But even though they are at odds in many ways, both Romantic and Modernist conceptions of authenticity focus on the artist as a creative individual and both remain oppositional towards mass culture, even if they work within it.

Of course, most genres of music and individual musicians will borrow from both of these threads, drifting back and forth or constructing a composite ideal. Black metal is no exception. As numerous critics and scholars have noted, black metal (and really all metal) embraces individual expression and boundary-breaking even as it remains committed to maintaining continuity with earlier styles. This duality can be seen clearly in Darkthrone's articulation of a self-conscious "black metal" style that bypassed the dominant metal aesthetics of the time by reaching back to a then-neglected core sound of the 1980s. Metalheads also generally maintain a strong sense of community and collective identity, even as some black metallers profess rather elitist views about those outside the scene, while reserving particularly strong contempt for those in the scene who they deem posers. Black metal's frequent focus on nature, ancient mythology, and imagined rural lifestyles also offers a clear echo of the Romantic ideology. The genre's growing popularity and visibility create the same sort of conundrum that has been faced by rock music more broadly, in that it is an "anti-mass culture" musical style that nonetheless commands a large audience.[24]

But this does not mean that black metallers are going to accept the genre's increased visibility and commercial success quietly, given that opposition to mainstream aesthetics forms so much of its DNA. This problem also gets particularly thorny because ideas of "authenticity" in popular music scenes often conflate a romanticized inner state of being with the aesthetic choices and standards that broadcast it to the world. Once these standards are defined and codified, however, they immediately become suspect because they can be easily adopted by anyone. Adopting a black metal identity, then, can become mostly a question of what you buy rather than a question of who you are. There is also perhaps a touch of the theological at work, a sort of inverted version of the Protestant *sola fide* doctrine: "One is not kvlt by works alone."[25] From a creative standpoint, concepts of authenticity also usually work as limiting devices that channel artistic creativity into predictable (and profitable) pathways. Indeed, the channeling and even self-censorship of artistic output is one of the essential functions of genre and subgenre categorizations. Yet, the sincerity crisis remains because authenticity is still, then, simply a matter of adhering to a set of predetermined artistic guidelines. Essentially, if "authentic" black metal sounds like Darkthrone, then, via the transitive property of grimness, it follows that a band that sounds like Darkthrone is authentic black metal. But anyone with experience within black metal scenes knows that it is never this simple; there is usually some sort of *je ne sais quoi* involved, if only as a shared consensus. Yet, given the amount of energy and vitriol spent arguing and defending authenticity within underground musical scenes, never-ending crisis may also work as a productive engine. It also gives music critics and academics like me a seemingly bottomless well of material to dissect, analyze, and "unpack."

Crucially, Norwegian black metal musicians also made claims to authenticity that are rooted in geography and location. This strategy perhaps found its first expression in the phrase "True Norwegian Black Metal," which was emblazoned on the back cover of Darkthrone's 1993 album *Under a Funeral Moon* and has become something of a rallying cry ever since. In this, they are not unlike other musical styles that utilize location as an authenticator, as seen variously in everything from Austin country musicians' opposition to Nashville, to 1990s grunge music's association with Seattle, to hip-hop's frequent invocation of locales down to the level of neighborhoods and streets. In nearly all of these instances, the geographic and economic distance from the major centers of the entertainment industry is a crucial component of their assertions of authenticity. In the case of Norway, there was clearly a desire to distinguish the Norwegian metal scene from Sweden, and Euronymous and Varg Vikernes were almost cartoonishly antagonistic towards the Swedish metal scene in their magazine profiles in the 1990s. To be sure, a significant part of the "True"-ness of Norwegian black metal relies on its anti-establishment rejection of the artistic and musical standards of the metal music industry at the time, and they promoted this as a mark of realness and authenticity. Yet these aesthetic ideals became not only a claim for being authentically metal, but also became an assertion of authentic Norwegian metalness. For listeners beyond Norway, it presented a new set of standards and expectations by which to judge bands' fidelity to both the black metal aesthetic and to their own Norwegianness. It is an assertion of locality and authenticity that binds the musical style to its place of origin, and further implies that black metal from other countries might be "false." The following chapter turns its attention to this sort of "musical geography," exploring how black metal's Nordic-ness informs both the creation and reception of this music.

2 "Where Cold Winds Blow"

'Where Cold Winds Blow' is another fast, freezing cold Black Metal song … ['The Pagan Winter'] possesses an epic feeling and produces mental images of traveling through a desolate wintry landscape, in the light of the full moon, on the way toward a cold grave. The Celtic Frost riffs near the end are well done, also … While Mayhem, Burzum and Immortal were all working on albums, Darkthrone was the first to release anything and were responsible for unleashing the fury from the north that would soon spread across the world, like an ancient plague.[1]

Nocturno and Zephyrous' riffs then are the freezing air from the coldest and darkest of places, biting your face as you walk along its changing drift.[2] **EXCERPTS FROM METAL-ARCHIVES REVIEWS OF *A BLAZE IN THE NORTHERN SKY*.**

In 2016, the Czech linguist and data scientist Jakub Marian created a "metal density" map of Europe that showed the number of metal bands in each country per one million people. Scandinavia far outpaced any of the other countries, with Finland scoring the top with 630 metal bands per one million people, followed by Sweden (428), Iceland (341), and Norway (299). These numbers included both active and inactive bands that were listed on the website *Encyclopedia Metallum*, a crowd-sourced archive of metal bands around the world. For comparison, the UK only had 68 metal bands per one million people, and the USA only 72, which is of course partly a function of their larger overall population size. Nevertheless, this map underscores the current perception of Scandinavia as a haven for heavy metal bands. Yet this situation is fairly recent. Prior to the emergence of black metal in Norway in the 1990s, heavy metal of all stripes was largely dominated by bands from the UK and USA. The UK, of course, has significant claims to the beginnings of heavy metal via Black Sabbath, Led Zeppelin, Deep Purple, and Motörhead, and many of the genre's idioms were further codified in the 1970s and 1980s by Judas Priest, Iron Maiden, and others. The USA contributed further to the genre via the thrash metal pioneers Metallica and Slayer as well as the glam metallers who came to dominate MTV in the latter half of the 1980s. Metal bands from outside the UK and USA who reached the upper tiers of the international music industry, such as Scorpions and Accept from Germany, were relatively rare. Even within the realms of extreme metal, many of the most visible acts in the late 1980s were American death metal bands like Death and Morbid Angel, alongside British bands like Bolt Thrower, Napalm Death, and Carcass.

In many ways, the story of Norwegian black metal shows how smaller localized metal scenes have carved out places for themselves within the international music industry over the last thirty years, often by using their local cultures as artistic and symbolic resources. In looking over articles and reviews of heavy metal bands, a band's nationality or geographic region is often referenced, even if it has little to do with their musical style. In some cases, there is also a fair bit of cultural stereotyping. For example, Finnish metal bands are almost invariably described as expressing their nation's supposed penchant for depression and alcoholism.[3] Often, reviewers and other writers make connections between metal bands and the environments and landscapes of their countries of origin. Consider that in the case of "sludge metal," the environment shows up in the genre's very name, as it is a style of slower and bluesier metal that happens to have been cultivated extensively by bands in Louisiana. Although "sludge" generally refers to the slower tempos and thick guitar tones of these bands, it also invokes the "sludge" of the swampy bayou.

Such relationships between music and geographic location have lately become objects of widespread scholarly interest, particularly in the face of intensifying cultural globalization. Assertions of local identity around the world have often come to symbolize an almost counter-cultural stance in this regard. In this vein, studies of Nordic music have recently begun to explore the idea of "borealism," which illustrates how Scandinavia and the North Atlantic regions have long been considered as an exotic borderland of continental Europe, only comparatively recently brought into its "civilized" fold. Scandinavia and the North Atlantic have often been romanticized as wild, magical, and uncivilized, simultaneously a realm of heroically violent Vikings, trolls and faeries, beautiful women, and "simple" provincial folk. In this way, the peoples of Scandinavia and the North Atlantic became an addition to the cast of "others" that the "civilized West" used as a means of exclusionary self-definition.[4]

This exotic perception of Scandinavia has had a long history. Consider, for example, the Hereford Mappa Mundi, a medieval map from the 1300s that features a Norwegian on skis at the edge of the world, which is otherwise populated with monsters and oddities. Centuries later, Enlightenment-era writers linked themselves to a mythical past via the epic tales of the *Nibelungenlied*, the Icelandic *Eddas*, and other Norse sagas, which they appropriated and anthologized. As a result, one of the hallmarks of borealism is that it brings the ancient world into modern times, often turning it into an imagined prelapsarian refuge from modern life. This sort of symbolic distancing takes on further political dimensions in the colonial histories of Norway, Iceland, and the Faroe Islands, all of which were once under the control of Denmark or Sweden, although with little of the brutal violence that was visited on European colonies elsewhere in the world.[5] Iceland, for its part, found itself in an enviable position because it was believed to hold the original and pure core version of its colonizer's culture in its language and epic poetry. By representing the past within the present, Iceland underscores the symbolic distance between the Nordic regions and the rest of "modern" Europe.

In the worlds of music, this exoticized conception of the North has manifested itself in everything from eighteenth-century collections of folk song that praised the "simplicity" and naivety of Nordic peoples to the romanticization of Icelandic culture and nature by fans of international stars like Björk and Sigur Rós.[6] Borealism figures heavily in musical tourism as well, as Iceland's promotional narratives regularly connect its music to geographies and folk beliefs, perhaps most obviously in the innumerable times over the years that the media has compared Björk to an elf or faerie. The 2007 Sigur Rós documentary and concert film *Heima* also directly connects the austere beauty of Sigur Rós's music with that of the stark Icelandic landscape by repeatedly cutting between concert footage of the band and gorgeous shots of glaciers, volcanic rock, and waterfalls.[7] Similarly, Faroese musicians highlight their geographic isolation,[8] and of course Norwegian black metal musicians fill their music videos, lyrics, and album covers with forests, fjords, and glaciers. The sights and sounds of nature are then perceived as both an expression of locality and a supposedly defining feature of indigenous music in the North. Nordic music, thus defined and classicized, then becomes a symbolic retreat from modernity.[9] Crucially, borealism encompasses not only the "outsider" vision of Nordic cultures, but also how these conceptions influence the ways in which Nordic people themselves view their homelands and their music. Indeed, the nineteenth-century national-romantic movements in Norway drew heavily on nature, Viking histories, and rural traditions in their quest to assert a Norwegian identity distinct from Denmark and Sweden, and this conception of "true" Norwegian-ness continues to echo and resonate today. Beyond Norway, other "small languages and cultures" of the Nordic regions become symbolic artistic resources in the global music market, as noted by Joshua Green in his study of Faroese musicians.[10] Given the prominence of violence in Norwegian black metal's past, black metal's particular flavor of musical borealism also relies on perceptions of the polar regions as full of unknown danger and primitive wildness. Beyond music, this idea crops up variously in books and films like *Frankenstein*, *The Call of the Wild*, *The Mountains of Madness*, *The Lord of the Rings*, and *Game of Thrones*, highlighting the fact that borealist ideas can extend to imaginary polar regions as well.

Although Norwegian national romantic art and literature frequently accentuate wilderness and rural living, Norwegians working with other popular genres of modern music rarely, if ever, rival black metal musicians' focus on their own Norwegian-ness. Similar references to Norwegian-ness seem largely absent among Norwegian musicians who perform other international genres like country, blues, electronica, and pop, in which they generally work within the accepted standard of the genre. For instance, many Norwegian country musicians go so far as to sing Norwegian lyrics with a Texas accent. Musicians working in popular regional styles like dansbandsmusik (which is typically a mix of sentimental "schlager" ballads, 1950s-style rock'n'roll, swing, country, and polka played by bands at dance halls) have little need to highlight their Nordic-ness since their audience is almost entirely centered in Scandinavia. However, Norwegian black metal was conceived from the beginning as a stylistic intervention aimed at the international metal underground. In its fetishization of Nordic landscapes and ancient Norse culture, black metal forged something that both speaks directly to Norwegians by referencing familiar touchstones of Norwegian identity, even as it also used its particular flavor of Nordic-ness as a symbolic challenge to the rest of the metal world.[11]

With this in mind, I've come to consider that Norwegian black metal interfaces with the same cultural dynamics and mythologies that underpinned the creation of the "world music" genre in the 1980s, along with numerous earlier examples of musical exoticism. Like many non-Western and regional musical styles, black metal's value for non-Nordic fans rests partly on its exotic aura of foreign otherness. In this regard, the promotion of Norwegian black metal has shared much with the way that music industries in global centers have long sold exotic sounds and imagery to their metropolitan audiences. Norwegian black metal's connection with world music may not be obvious at first, but they share a number of the same marketing strategies and conceptual affinities. Like world music genres, Norwegian black metal has often highlighted its connections to nature, local histories, magical and religious traditions, and even indigenous resistance (in the form of church arsons). As the ethnomusicologist Timothy Taylor has noted, the world music industry of the 1980s–2000s often promoted an ideal of cultural and musical primitiveness and purity, focusing on traditional musical styles that were allegedly untouched by Western capitalism.[12] For

Western listeners, these recordings were basically exoticized escapist fantasies, with their presumed authenticity resting on their lack of overt commercial intent and the absence of identifiable influence from Western popular music. The musicologist Simon Frith has argued that the "difference" that was being marketed in world music wasn't so much between Western and non-Western music but instead, "between real and artificial sounds, between the musically true and the musically false, between authentic and inauthentic musical experiences."[13] In many cases, however, the musicians on these records were consciously tailoring their music to meet these expectations, quite possibly at the behest of the record labels' marketing divisions. Rather than representing the music that people in these regions perform and experience as a part of their daily lives, world music recordings effectively presented a simulacrum of local music traditions in order to satisfy audiences in Europe and the USA. They promised these listeners an authentic and unfiltered musical window to a supposedly simpler and less commercialized world, and went to great lengths to deliver on that promise.

The visual presentation of *A Blaze in the Northern Sky* is a case in point, as it self-consciously rejects the accepted artwork standards of metal releases in the early 1990s and provided a model for many albums to follow. At a time when the artwork of extreme metal albums was getting increasingly intricate and vivid, Darkthrone opted for a grainy black-and-white photo of their rhythm guitarist Zephyrous with their logo in the corner and a simple typeface for the album's title. The photo is so dark and of such poor resolution that almost all that can be discerned is Zephyrous's corpse-painted face floating in murky blackness, appearing like a screaming apparition. The rear cover features the tracklist and similarly grainy black-and-white photos of the three band members in corpsepaint. Fenriz is sitting in a forest, almost as if meditating or in a trance, Zephyrous again appears to be screaming, while Nocturno Culto grimaces menacingly from behind a large cross. Underneath their portraits, Fenriz is credited with "Percussion, Satanic Poetry and Haunting Chants" while Nocturno Culto performs "Lead Guitar and Voice (of The Night)." The inner sleeve includes the dedication, "*A Blaze in the Northern Sky* is eternally dedicated to the king of black/death metal underground; namely Euronymous!," recording and design credits, and finishes with the statement "Darkthrone plays *Unholy Black Metal* exclusively."

The overall visual aesthetic of the album is effectively that of a demo recording, a DIY ideal that Darkthrone continued to cultivate in their following albums as well. It looks like something that would have been quickly whipped up at a local printing shop and duplicated on a photocopier rather than a product coming from a well-established record label. The low-resolution photos combined with the use of corpsepaint create an aura of mystery around these musicians, and their exaggerated poses make them seem a little unhinged. When combined with the sensationalistic interviews with Euronymous and Vikernes published in subsequent years, that seems to have been the point. Similar to the musical aspects discussed in the previous chapter, the artwork on *A Blaze in the Northern Sky* is also a revivalist affair, recalling the cheap packaging, photography, and costuming of the first releases by Bathory and Celtic Frost. It's also worth noting that black-and-white photos like these were typical of underground metal zines at the time, as opposed to the full-color glossy photo spreads in higher-profile music magazines.

Darkthrone's DIY aesthetic and claim of musical exclusiveness argues for a similar kind of authenticity and musical purity that is untouched by commercialism. Further, the "cheap" look of the record plays into the borealistic concept of Norway as a kind of provincial backwater. Although it's meant as a rejection of commercialism and a signal of fidelity to Darkthrone's 1980s forebears, this visual aesthetic quickly became a norm in itself. The years that followed saw numerous black metal bands opting for low-resolution black-and-white portraits of themselves out in nocturnal forests or next to ruined castles, often with medieval weaponry or torches. The color palette for any other photos and text is often stark black and white. All told, Darkthrone's nostalgic visual concept ultimately became a hallmark of black metal, both in Norway and beyond. To this day, it remains an assertion of artistic dedication to the black metal style, rather than just implying that the band couldn't afford to hire a professional photographer or print their cover art in color.

Even beyond Darkthrone, there remains a desire among many black metal fans (and metal scholars) to insulate black metal from the forces of commerce and romanticize its supposed independence from the music industry. The genre's cultivation beyond the usual urban centers of the music industry, sometimes in circumstances of extreme isolation, forms a key component of this ideal. For example, Darkthrone's current rehearsal and recording studio is an isolated cabin in the Norwegian forest, and black metal musicians from fellow Norwegian Gaahl (Gorgoroth, Gaahl's Wyrd) to the American band Wolves in the Throne Room regularly promote rural lifestyles. We'll see later that this ideal of isolation figures heavily in the borealistic ideal of black metal.

At the time that Darkthrone was recording *A Blaze in the Northern Sky*, it seems that they and other Norwegian metal bands were beginning to understand the international currency of their cultural heritage. As noted earlier, the international metal underground was focused on the English-speaking world prior to black metal's rise to prominence. As a result, most European bands (along with bands from Asia and South America) adopted English band names and wrote their lyrics in English. The emergence of the Norwegian black metal scene changed the environment in the metal music industry, showing the potential for metal to interface with more localized cultures. By the mid-1990s, several Norwegian bands had released albums that explored ancient Nordic identities, most notably Enslaved's *Vikingligr Veldi* (1994), which was sung in old Icelandic, and Ulver's *Bergtatt* (1995), an album in Norwegian exploring tales of Norwegian mountain trolls.[14] Darkthrone's first foray into Norwegian-language lyrics was "Inn I De Dype Skogers Fabn" ("In the Deep Forest's Embrace") from *Under a Funeral Moon* (1993), but the following album *Transilvanian Hunger* (1994) included only one song in English. From the bands' point of view, some of them simply thought that black metal vocals in Norwegian sounded "cool," but others considered it a point of local or national pride. The Norwegian black metal scene's antagonism towards the Swedish metal scene likely also played a role. From the non-Norwegian listener's perspective, it made the often-indecipherable vocals of black metal that much more alien and uncanny because the lyric sheets (if provided) were no longer of much help.

"We Rode with the North Wind"

Discussing music in any forum often involves the use of metaphors, partly because the vocabulary of music theory is often impenetrable to the majority of listeners (even if they understand more than they typically think), but also because that jargon inevitably falls short of describing the music's effects. It might describe what the music *does*, but it is unable to account for the full aural experience, which engages not only senses of hearing but also the imagination. For black metal, that aspect of the music is often filled in with geographic and environmental metaphors, allowing black metal's lyrical and visual conceits to imprint themselves on the experience of the musical sound itself. Even though Darkthrone and their fellow black metallers might have been interested in reviving the aesthetics of the 1980s "first wave" in their music and artwork, they also added another important ingredient to the mix with their fascination with Nordic environments and their own Norse-ness. In the years following, black metal lyrics became notoriously full of cold winds, frozen mountains, and forests populated with wolves, trolls, and other mythical denizens of the wild. The album art often features shots of imposing fjords, misty forests, and snow-covered mountains, and early music videos by Emperor and Immortal featured the band members performing in forests and triumphantly raising their guitars on top of mountains. The color palette of album art also heavily favors "cool" colors like blues, greens, and violets rather than "warmer" reds and oranges. And, of course, *A Blaze in the Northern Sky* makes its Northern-ness explicit in its very title, a phrase which would likely be assumed to be a reference to aurora borealis in most other contexts.

It is almost a cliché at this point to refer to black metal as sounding "cold" or "grim," but the fact that the music is commonly discussed in these terms is significant. Black metal record reviewers and bloggers regularly refer to forests, mountains, and fog in their reviews and articles, likely taking cues from the bands' lyrics and cover art. Part of this tendency is no doubt just a function of metal reviewers' natural tendencies towards florid language, born out of the need to draw distinctions between dozens of bands whose music might be largely indistinguishable. Yet, the pervasiveness of these environmental and geographical metaphors suggests that for many listeners the musical and sonic gestures of black metal can function almost as a musical evocation of the Nordic and polar regions.

Although Norwegian black metal's fascination with wilderness environments was certainly a new development in metal music, it has several important forebears within music and art. In particular, black metal's focus on nature can be usefully understood as an echo of the cultural and philosophical currents that underpinned Romanticism in the eighteenth to nineteenth centuries. Although Romanticism had many flavors across Europe and the Americas, in broad terms it developed in reaction to the focus on rationality during the Enlightenment, and also as a response to the social dislocations of the Industrial Revolution. In Romantic-era literature, music, and artwork, the notion of turning one's back on the world in order to explore one's own inner mysteries is a recurring theme. This introspective journey is often facilitated by solitude in nature, and the natural world can reflect the journey itself. For example, in Mary Shelley's *Frankenstein*, Victor Frankenstein finds himself rejuvenated by solo sojourns into the mountains, while the alpine wilderness also provides his creature with protection from society. A famous musical example of this idea would be Franz Schubert's *Winterreise* (1828), a song cycle that features an alienated lover traversing a wintry landscape that reflects his own inner sorrow. The archetypal Romantic hero is a man who is estranged from society and living an isolated existence, but with a sense of nobility and authenticity; his isolated life of solitary introspection is society's loss rather than the other way around. It's worth noting that in nearly every case the Romantic hero is a man; women were almost never afforded the opportunity to be a brooding loner. This literary archetype had philosophical echoes as well, particularly among the American transcendentalist philosophers Ralph Waldo Emerson and Henry David Thoreau. Emerson in particular considered communion with nature as a spiritual encounter with the divine, which could only be accessed in solitude.[15] Thoreau built on these themes in *Walden*, using his two-year stay at an isolated cabin as a means for critiquing society's materialism and arguing for a spiritual awakening via a self-reliant and simplistic life as a part of nature.

Certainly, the individualism of Romanticism informs black metal's ethos, along with its rejections of society in favor of the "wholeness" of nature. In truth, the Romantic ideal of the artist as nonconformist outsider who challenges society's norms has informed so much twentieth-century popular music from blues, to jazz, to rock, and even country, that its re-expression in black metal seems rather mundane. Yet, black metal's adulation of wilderness allows it to more fully inherit the Romantics' fetishization of nature, as well as other aspects. In particular, Romantic-era artists and musicians were often fascinated with the concept of the "sublime," an aesthetic category articulated by Edmund Burke in his 1757 treatise *A Philosophical Inquiry into the Origin of Our Ideas of the Sublime and Beautiful*.[16] As formulated by Burke and later expounded on by other philosophers, the "sublime" refers to a state of awe or astonishment when faced with unknown vastness and infinity. Although feelings of fear or terror are a crucial component to the sublime, it isn't necessarily an unpleasant experience. Archetypal situations for experiencing the sublime are standing at the edge of a precipice or looking into the night sky in an area devoid of light pollution, both of which remind us of our individual vulnerability and insignificance. In the Romantic era, the vast landscape paintings of Caspar David Friedrich or Albert Bierstadt provide a clear representation of the concept, and also signal a new aesthetic appreciation of mountainous landscapes in these terms. It's no coincidence that black metal bands regularly utilize these sorts of landscape paintings in their album artwork. Black metal musicians also invoke the sublime lyrically in the genre's numerous references to forests, mountains, and cosmic vastness; Emperor's *In the Nightside Eclipse* (1994) provides several excellent examples. Beyond lyrics, one could also find the concept of the sublime articulated in black metal's maximalist sonic ideal, in which the wall of unrelenting sound from the guitars and drums often threatens to overwhelm the vocals in the mix.[17]

In his 2018 dissertation, the historian Christopher Thompson has drawn a number of parallels between Norwegian black metal musicians' interaction with their country's landscapes and Norway's self-definition as a nation and distinct culture.[18] These connections provide further examples of how borealism can inform not only perceptions abroad but also shape the identities of Nordic peoples, particularly when that identity is intimately associated with the landscape. Forests and mountains not only convey feelings of remoteness or majesty, they also seem primordial and timeless, serving as symbols for an idealized "Norwegian-ness" that is similarly unchanging and enduring. The forbidding frozen wilderness of black metal likewise mirrors an idealized Norwegian spirit of perseverance and toughness, both in terms of the ability to live within such landscapes and to tame them for agrarian use. It seems productive to consider the self-professed "trueness" of Norwegian black metal as a reflection of this sort of masculine exceptionalism. As an American, I also can't help but draw parallels with the privileged place the cowboys of the American West have long held in our own romanticized national narrative and sense of identity. Magical and mythical elements remain important, however, expressed particularly in the paintings and drawings of trolls and other mythical beings by the artist Theodor Kittlesen (1857–1914). In these works, the boundary between the landscape and those beings is often blurred so it seems as if the forests and mountains themselves are enchanted and alive. Several Norwegian black metal bands, including Burzum, Ulver, and Satyricon, have used Kittlesen's work as cover art, and his distinctive style is easily recognizable for many Norwegians, making it yet another aspect of black metal that builds on existing touchstones of Norwegian identity.

This borealist vision of Norway as a wild and magical place is of course rife with ironies. Most obvious is that Norway is one of the wealthiest countries in the world thanks to the massive oil reserves it controls in the North Sea. This wealth provides for an incredibly high standard of living along with robust welfare, pension, and healthcare systems. In keeping with the ethos of Nordic social democracy, the Norwegian government also provides support for a wide range of musical and artistic activities by providing grants or other subsidies. Indeed, one of the smaller media scandals in the midst of the tabloid frenzy around black metal in the 1990s was the fact that some of the bands had evidently received a stipend to help them rent a rehearsal space. Further, the scene certainly would not have gotten as much traction as it did were it not for the parents of Varg Vikernes and Euronymous, who provided funding for recording and helped bankroll the record store Helvete. With this in mind, the fact that these Norwegian black metallers repeatedly condemned the comforts of modern society in interviews in the 1990s feels a bit hypocritical, even though it's not all that surprising. After all, one of the side perks of living in relative comfort is the privilege of yearning for pariah-hood and hardship.

The alignment of black metal's musical style with images of wilderness and nature also informs much of the global black metal scene, even among bands who don't explicitly invoke the coldness and darkness of Nordic or polar regions. Solitude and wilderness remain central lyrical conceits for many bands, even if only as a symbolic rejection of modern society or an atavistic fantasy. For example, in the United States, bands from the "Cascadian" scene in the Pacific Northwest like Wolves in the Throne Room, Blood of the Black Owl, and Fauna write lengthy songs about ritualized transformations into forest creatures, ecological catastrophes, and mankind's return to the wilderness. Rather than referencing the mythical beings of the Nordic wilderness, these bands often seem to draw additional inspiration from new-age and neopagan religious movements, along with hints of American Indian spiritualities. A representative lyric from Wolves in the Throne Room reads, "I will lay down my bones among the rocks and roots of the deepest hollow next to the streambed. The quiet hum of the earth's dreaming is my new song. When I awake, the world will be born anew." Many of these black metal bands build on the concept of the sublime by exploring the idea of a non-anthropocentric world, a world without humans or in which human life is incidental or secondary to that of other forest denizens and spirits. Black metal's misanthropic and anti-modern invocation of the wilderness then becomes not only a potential refuge from modernity but also a yearning for a return to some kind of primordial formlessness or oblivion. The self is dissolved, either ceremonially or through natural processes of decay and rot.[19] Yet, when these Cascadian bands write on such things, the intent in the lyrics often points to a desire for cleansing and healing via the natural world, as opposed to the emphases on cold, dark, and even malevolent landscapes found in many other black metal lyrics. These American black metal musicians adapted the Norwegians' focus on the natural world to their own ends, as reflections of their distinct desires and wildernesses.

"Summon my Warriors ..."

For many of the Norwegian bands, however, the environments and landscapes of wild Norway are explicitly connected with pre-modern and pre-Christian Norwegian cultures. Although Darkthrone don't seem to have as much interest in Vikings as some of their compatriots, they are central to any discussion of borealism. In modern media, Vikings have often been utilized as a sort of all-purpose barbarian, portrayed variously as violently brutal thugs or as honorable and spiritual warriors. As with most modern reincarnations of ancient figures, their portrayals shift according to the demands of the present. The relative lack of reliable written accounts of Viking culture perhaps also makes Vikings uniquely flexible, although the existence of extensive documentation has never really hindered creative and anachronistic reuses of historical figures and ancient cultures.

The Norwegian band Enslaved in particular has cultivated an intense interest in Viking culture, occasionally utilizing archaic dialects in their songs. Enslaved have also been instrumental in the creation of the Midgardsblot metal festival, an outdoor concert, religious gathering, and symposium held at a Viking archeological site. However, the Swedish death metal band Amon Amarth has probably taken this concept the farthest, as their albums and music videos are full of Viking imagery, and their stage show features drum risers fashioned as a Viking longboat and a Viking helmet. Amon Amarth's singer also co-owns an online shop entitled Grimfrost that specializes in all sorts of Viking-themed merchandise, including drinking horns, books, armor, jewelry, beard accessories, historical clothing, along with the usual assortment of shirts, hoodies, and hats. Almost everything is adorned with runes and Thor's Hammers. Beyond metal, the neo-folk groups Heilung and Wardruna treat their concerts as modern interpretations of ancient Viking rituals and music, often featuring elaborate costumes and archaic instruments.

Yet, in many black metal songs, this Viking or pre-Christian nostalgia takes on a millenarian tone, indulging in reveries of reconquest that would re-establish Nordic wilderness and the ancient cultures that went along with it. This is one of the main lyrical themes running through *A Blaze in the Northern Sky*. The opening song, "Kathaarian Life Code," revels in apocalyptic and Biblical imagery while the title references the Cathars, a heretical Christian group based in southern France that challenged the authority of the Catholic church in the Middle Ages until they were wiped out in the Albigensian Crusade in the early thirteenth century. The song ends with an invocation of "Kathaaria," a heretical and diabolical world that will rise after this apocalypse. "In the Shadow of the Horns" refers specifically to a "New Millenium" that will usher in a new dark age like one "only seen by the Kings of the Dawn (of the) First Millennium." "A Blaze in the Northern Sky" imagines a type of apocalypse in which the sky turns black, the sun dies, and a "northern storm" takes over the landscape. The song refers to the thousand years that passed between the birth of Jesus and the Christianization of Scandinavia in the ninth to eleventh centuries in the lines "It took ten times a hundred Years / Before the King on the Northern Throne was brought / Tales of the crucified one," noting that a thousand years "of lost pride and lust" have passed since then. The song ends with the lines, "We are a blaze in the northern sky / The next thousand years are OURS," which provocatively marks the beginning of the new dark age in the present. A number of the songs on *A Blaze in the Northern Sky* also invoke infernal spiritual communities like the "coven of forgotten delight" and the "race of cursed seeds," a lyrical practice that is also mirrored in countless liner note dedications and shout-outs that laud the black metal community.[20] As a further example beyond Darkthrone, the band Kampfar's 1998 song "Norse" describes pagan ancestors calling through white waterfalls and dark and misty forests, and a later verse calls for fields and homes to become fire and blood and for lambs to become wolves once again. This song also makes a reference to the thousand-year-old Christianization of Norway, and the symbolism of "lambs" becoming "wolves" underscores this point. The fact that this was, at the time, the only song Kampfar had recorded in English also indicates that this expression of Norse pride, tied to the environment, was meant to be clearly understood by audiences beyond Norway.

However, this focus on violent and apocalyptic cultural reconquest brings with it a number of potentially alarming subtexts. For example, the Oslo band Satyricon's 1996 song "Mother North" personifies the polar North as a spirit that will return and exact retribution. The lyrics of "Mother North" are somewhat oblique, but the opening line "Mother North – how can they sleep while their beds are burning" is a clear play on the chorus of the Australian band Midnight Oil's 1987 song "Beds are Burning." However, Satyricon flip the line, as the original reads, "How can *we* sleep while *our* beds are burning." "Beds are Burning" was originally written in support of returning ancestral lands to Australian Aboriginal populations, with the burning bed seeming to function as a metaphor for collective colonial guilt on the part of white Australians. In Satyricon's refashioning, however, the line effectively casts the North as having been colonized, and even though the lyrics are somewhat vague, the xenophobic undercurrent of the song is undeniable. Further, Darkthrone's "Over fjell og gjennom torner" ("Over the mountain and through the thorns") from *Transilvanian Hunger* concludes with the lines "Den Norrøne Rase må Slakte den andre / Nar blåmenn dunker for tungt pa var dør," which translates roughly as "The Norse race must slaughter the other / when Blue-men pound too heavily on our door," with "blue-men" apparently being a medieval Scandinavian term for Moors and other dark-skinned peoples. Although the controversy around *Transilvanian Hunger* revolved mostly around the statement "Norsk Arisk Black Metal" on its back cover and the band's ill-conceived press release, this lyric takes that racist subtext and simply makes it "text," at least for Scandinavians. To my knowledge, Darkthrone have never addressed this particular lyric, which is not that surprising given the obscurity of the reference and the existence of much more public controversies around *Transilvanian Hunger.*

As noted in the introduction, Fenriz has repeatedly disavowed these sentiments and expressed regret over them in the years since, claiming that they came from a place of pain and anger with his life at the time, but *Transilvanian Hunger* remains a prime example of how black metal's penchant for provocation can easily slip into (or simply unmask) racism and xenophobia. Even beyond black metal, borealism's tendency to link present concerns with the mythologized past highlights the ways that past has been idealized and weaponized both by historical Nazis and present-day white nationalists. The romanticized notions of wilderness and solitude at the core of black metal borealism easily function as a code for criticizing the ethnic diversity of cosmopolitan urban areas, and its gauzy view of imagined pastoral pasts finds numerous parallels with fascist iconographies of the twentieth century. Invocations of Vikings and warriors also underscore the reactionary gender politics that often accompany such nostalgic worldviews, hearkening back to a time when gender identities and roles were supposedly clearly articulated and accepted. Given the symbolic currency of "the North" within white nationalist discourse, it's unfortunately probably not that surprising to find fantasies of masculine dominance, ethnic homogeneity, and cultural chauvinism worming through the borealistic conceptions of black metal's global scene. Even in the absence of overt racism or nationalism, these essentialized conceptions of Nordic history and identity in black metal often work to reinforce exclusive ethnic boundaries on Norwegian-ness.[21] In general, ethno-nationalism's main rhetorical strategy is usually to tie ethnic and cultural identity to geography and the environment via "blood and soil" rhetoric. This is not always a prominent or visible thread in Norwegian black metal's borealistic appeal across the globe, but it would be an act of willful ignorance to pretend that it's not always potentially lurking underneath the surface.

For those metalheads who are involved in radical white nationalism, these nostalgic and romanticized visions of Scandinavian cultural traditions figure heavily in their racist and xenophobic worldviews.[22] Norse symbols are regularly used by these groups, and as such it can be difficult to discern whether someone is a neo-Nazi, a practitioner of a modern heathen religion like Ásatrú, a die-hard Amon Amarth fan, or some combination of the three. For radical nationalist groups, the ability to conceal their expressions within existing symbols is certainly part of the point. But while there certainly is an argument to be made that symbols or musical styles are forever tainted if white nationalists get a hold of them, some black metal bands and scenes (along with some Ásatrú and neopagan communities) are actively pursuing and cultivating a consciously diverse and inclusive vision of the genre in the hopes of unmooring it from associations with right-wing extremism.

However, these utilizations of Scandinavian culture necessarily take on different implications in different cultures and scenarios. Indeed, Scandinavians who are not involved in metal or heathenry might find it all a bit silly, almost like a musical equivalent of the cheesy Viking trinkets and souvenirs sold in gift shops at airports and tourist traps. Even among fans, some likely approach it in the same spirit as cosplayers at science-fiction conventions or medieval fairs; it's a chance as an adult to play dress-up and to compare costumes in fellowship with other fans. However, many participants also experience these elements as a crucial facet of a cultural identity that involves the practice of heathen religious traditions, with black metal music acting as an expression of worship or a tool for initiation.[23] Musicians and fans who are not Scandinavian participate as well; the "Nordicness" of black metal is something that is regularly adopted by fans worldwide and likely even grows in importance for non-Nordic audiences.[24] For American fans who are descended from Scandinavian immigrants in particular, this metal borealism can also provide a sense of rootedness and shared heritage, although this can obviously make for a slippery slope. In a sense, black metal almost acts like a diasporic music connecting these American fans to an imagined homeland full of wild landscapes, seafaring adventures, and mystical spirituality, as opposed to the mundanity of American suburbia. In this respect, the exoticisms at work in Norwegian black metal differ from those within the milieu of "world music." Rather than seeking an experience of exotic "otherness" via music from a faraway land, these American black metal fans are instead finding exoticized versions of themselves in this music from Norway. Of course, the Norway that is often portrayed in black metal is a fantasy not far removed from Tolkein's *Lord of the Rings*, which obviously fired the imaginations of many of these Norwegian musicians in their teenage years and which I should note also carries its own masculinist and racist subtexts. But for many black metal fans around the world looking for the North in their music, this romanticized vision of Norway as uncultivated and wild, but also honorable and spiritual (although not Christian), is what they will open their wallets for.

Tourism

In his 1996 article "From Pilgrim to Tourist – Or a Short History of Identity," the sociologist Zygmunt Bauman described the "tourist's world" as one in which "the strange is tame, domesticated, and no longer frightens; shocks come in a package deal with safety."[25] This tourist's world is the final stop in our exploration of borealism, in which black metal becomes a part of Norway's cultural self-definition, even though most Norwegians are certainly not black metal fans. Norway has become a "metal country" whether they like it or not. Certain places in Norway have become bona-fide black metal tourist attractions, notably the site of Euronymous's store Helvete, which is now a black metal record store and museum called Neseblod, after years as a coffee shop and bakery. Fans can go down to the basement and take a photo with the "black metal" graffiti they've seen in several iconic photos from the 1990s. The rebuilt Fantoft church in Bergen is a similarly popular tourist site, because, as the saying goes, there are few tourist attractions that can compare with a crime scene. When I traveled to Bergen in 2015, I dutifully took the train to Fantoft, walked the short distance to the church, took a few metal-looking selfies in front of it, and posted them to Facebook as soon as possible: +25 Kvlt Points. The popularity of these two sites is not accidental: they are both quite photo-friendly and figure heavily in imagery from the 1990s scene. Euronymous's old apartment building or the spot in the woods where Bård "Faust" Eithun stabbed Magne Andreasson to death (assuming one could find it) aren't nearly as recognizable and would also make for rather more somber experiences. Helvete and Fantoft allow for a selective memorialization based on familiar images and locations, ultimately feeling rather like visiting a location that featured in a favorite movie or television show.

It is also worth noting that the murders and arsons of the Black Circle also became more widely known just as the publishing world was discovering a lucrative market in

Scandinavian crime fiction, otherwise known as "Nordic Noir." In the first decades of the twenty-first century, Nordic noir books like Stieg Larsson's *Girl with the Dragon Tattoo* series became incredibly popular in Anglophone markets, while television series like the Danish *Forbrydelsen* (*The Killing*) and the Danish/Swedish *The Bridge* were remade in American and British contexts. Although these crime narratives clearly follow existing models for noir fiction, they often feature dark and snowy Nordic landscapes and isolated provincial settings. The murders in these books and films are also often shockingly cruel, with tranquil villages and prosperous modern Nordic cities serving as ironic backdrops for brutal violence. But the scholar Jakob Stougaard-Nielsen has noted that in the case of Nordic noir, the sense of exoticism is muted because Nordic societies and cultures are depicted in ways that feel familiar and accessible to Anglophone audiences.[26] Nordic noir offers the attraction and allure of the foreign without the disorientation of more immersive encounters with foreign cultures. There's more than a little of this vibe in the story of the Norwegian Black Circle, a group of young middle-class musicians living in comparative affluence, thanks to the generosity of their parents and their government, who suddenly began engaging in acts of terroristic arson and murderous violence. It is honestly rather surprising that it took until 2019 for the whole tragicomedy of Varg Vikernes and Euronymous to come to the big screen as a feature film.

Beyond tourist sites, Norway has also embraced black metal as a part of its official musical and artistic culture. The museum of Norwegian popular music, Rockheim, has a room dedicated to black metal that features videos and artifacts related to the music. Several art museums have curated exhibits of black metal artwork or art inspired by black metal.

In 2014, the Norwegian government commissioned black metal musicians Ivar Bjørnson (Enslaved) and Einar Selvik (Wardruna) to write and perform a piece in commemoration of the 200th anniversary of the Norwegian constitution at the Eidsivablot festival in Eidsvoll, Norway. In 2013, the Royal Norwegian Ministry of Culture established Music Norway, a consulting and grant-awarding organization dedicated to promoting Norwegian music abroad. Although Music Norway concerns itself with all sorts of music, they regularly promote black metal and have sponsored international black metal tours by Mayhem, Enslaved, Taake, and others. This sort of institutional support obviously raises the question of whether it runs counter to the transgressive ideal that forms much of the genre's appeal, but such domestication is at the heart of the process of recuperation described in the previous chapter. For those Norwegian black metallers who play their music professionally, being embraced by their country's official cultural institutions is probably a small price to pay. Finally, as impenetrable as the music might be for non-metalheads, black metal's love of Norwegian landscapes, wilderness, and history mirrors the outdoor focus of most Norwegian tourism. After all, the stunning geography of the country remains its most valuable tourist resource, and black metal only adds to the country's borealistic mystique. Given that the outdoorsy and "Vikingy" tone of most Norwegian tourism dovetails with black metal's imagery and lyrics, it seems like a productive alliance even if some of black metal's more underground-minded fans might bristle at the notion.

In wrapping up, it is worth a final note that my comparison of black metal borealism with the imperatives of world music exoticism and tourism can surely extend beyond Scandinavia. The pressure to conform to exotic stereotypes is likely also felt keenly by metal musicians in Eastern Europe, Latin America and the Caribbean, South America, Africa, Asia, and the Middle East. For metal bands in these regions, there is also often an implied expectation on the part of the global listenership that they perform their nationality or ethnicity within their music. Accomplishing this often involves utilizing local instruments or costumes in one way or another as a way to highlight their local identity, usually with an emphasis on pre-modern or agrarian life that is similar to that found in Scandinavian black metal.[27] However, bands who play in styles like thrash metal or death metal may find themselves at a disadvantage because their music might not as readily broadcast its place of origin.[28] Although metal is a clearly globalized form of music that bridges cultural divides and connects people across the world, metal musicians in these countries who have ambitions in the Anglophone music industry may find themselves needing to put on a cultural pageant of sorts, even if they might rather just shred like everybody else.

3 "Paragon Belial"

Beyond its novel fascination with Norwegian culture and Nordic environments, Norwegian black metal also introduced a new musical and sonic aesthetic to metal, one which promised to go beyond death metal, which was at the time considered the apex of heaviness. This "blackening" of metal formed partly as a response to the fact that when American and Swedish death metal reigned over the metal underground in the early 1990s, there seemed to be nowhere to turn to for more heaviness.[1] Turning towards lighter fare would have been an unconscionable sellout and an implicit admission of failure. Earlier in Chapter 1, I discussed how *A Blaze in the Northern Sky* is at heart a revivalist record, drawing inspiration from the punkish simplicity of underground 1980s metal. But it is important to consider what this revival meant in its historical context. The first black metal albums by Darkthrone, Mayhem, and others not only pointed out a new path for metal but also argued for a radical reassessment of metal's past. Not incidentally, in doing so they also stitched together the notion of a "first wave" of black metal that retroactively formed their lineage. The bands in this lineage, however, were ones that had been largely dismissed by many metal fans due to their sloppy musicianship, simplistic and repetitive songwriting, and amateurish recording production. By reclaiming bands like Bathory, Hellhammer, Venom, and the obscure California band Von as the standard-bearers of "true" metal, Darkthrone and their compatriots located heaviness in music that had been previously neglected, creating a counter-narrative to the musical aesthetics that birthed death metal. In doing so, they opened the world of underground metal up to a number of alternative ideas.[2] This chapter focuses particularly on the musical and sonic aesthetic of black metal in *A Blaze in the Northern Sky* and beyond, in terms of the genre's musical idioms and sonic signature. Since *A Blaze in the Northern Sky* still retains vestiges of Darkthrone's earlier death metal phase, it is an ideal album for exploring how metal got blackened.

Approaching aspects of musical style in any genre does require some clarifications, however. My concern in this chapter is mostly with "nuts and bolts" characteristics of Darkthrone's musical style, as a way to explore the things that set their black metal style apart from death metal and thrash metal. In some academic circles, this is kind of an "old school" approach in that my defining characteristics deal mostly with the notes that the musicians are playing, the way in which they are playing them, and how those performances are recorded. In a lot of ways, my approach is informed by Robert Walser's 1993 book *Running with the Devil* and Glen Pillsbury's book *Damage Incorporated: Metallica and the Production of Musical Identity.*[3] Determining what particular music *means* has long been an incredibly dicey and contested proposition, but I always prefer to include concrete aspects of the music and its recording in addition to exploring how those aspects are interpreted by listeners. Beyond my training as a musical academic, a lot of this perspective comes from playing extreme metal, in which I and my fellow musicians often experience the performance of songs as a series of physically demanding musical tests that hopefully add up to something artistically meaningful in the end. There are, of course, many other ways to derive meaning from music ranging from deep dives into music theory, ethnomusicological studies of local musical practices, reception histories, and other perspectives. My intention in this chapter is to explore some distinctive musical gestures that show up in *A Blaze in the Northern Sky* and in later black metal records, becoming a sort of sonic signature for the style in years to come.

Blackened Harmonies

Although I suspect that most readers will be familiar with aspects of heavy metal musical style, there are a few key musical concepts within heavy metal that black metal builds upon, so a brief exposition might be helpful. In terms of harmony and melody, heavy metal is known for its extensive use of tritones, a musical interval that is notable for its extreme dissonance. From a technical standpoint, a tritone interval is separated by three whole steps, which puts it equidistant between octaves. For example, if one starts from middle C on a piano, the tritone F# is the same number of steps away on the keyboard regardless of whether one goes to the F# above or below C.

Most systems of harmony rely on one pitch serving as a central pillar to hold up a musical "key," but the tritone destabilizes this concept because it doesn't seem to lead anywhere. Consequently, neither the major nor the minor scale include a tritone, and classical music theory is very strict about its use. However, this sense of instability resulted in a long history of tritones being used as musical symbols for the demonic and strange, particularly in opera and film music.

Probably the most familiar example is the stereotypical "tying-the-girl-to-the-train-tracks" music found in numerous old movies and cartoons. The tritone interval appears in heavy metal from the very beginning in the genre-defining first song on the first Black Sabbath album, "Black Sabbath," in which the main riff consists of an octave and a tritone repeated obsessively, resulting in a claustrophobic, unsettling, and "evil" sound.[4]

Beyond tritones, the signature heavy metal harmony is the "power chord," a two- or three-note chord in which the guitarist plays only the root note of the chord, and the fifth above (or fourth below), and often the octave above the root note.

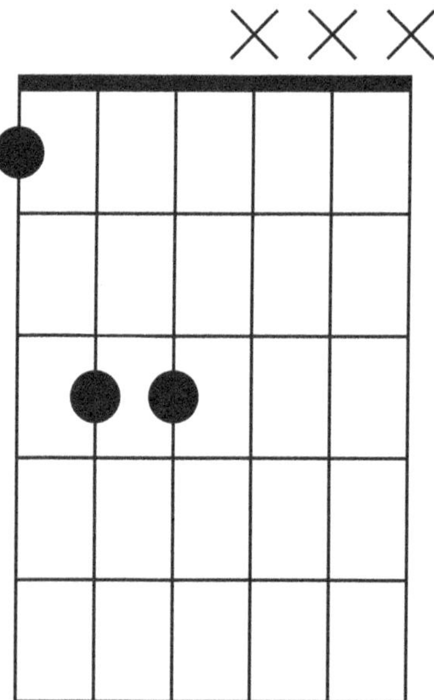

Example 3.1 *Power chord played on first fret (F).*

Because they have only the root and the perfect fifth, power chords are neither major nor minor. In many musical contexts this results in an open, transparent, and resonant sound, often used to evoke spaciousness, as in the opening of Alexander Courage's opening theme music for the original *Star Trek* series. The root and open fifth is also a characteristic sound that is used as an underpinning drone in bagpipe music and in classical Indian music. Metal does a few special things with the idea, though. For one, when played under heavy distortion, power chords generate a subharmonic tone an octave below the root note, giving an impression of bigness and weight. The power chord shape shown above is also commonly moved up and down the neck of the guitar as a fundamental part of many metal riffs. Parallel motion of octaves and fifths is anathema for traditional classical voice-leading, but this sort of chord-shape movement is idiomatic and intuitive on a guitar. Essentially, power chords make a single-note riff sound "bigger" without getting in the way of its melodic contour. If you are a guitarist or you have access to a guitarist, playing either "Smoke on the Water" or "Iron Man" first as single-note riffs and then as proper power chords will clearly demonstrate this effect.

Black metal bands retain power chords as a fundamental technique, but over the 1990s a number of black metal bands began to explore the use of fully voiced triads in place of power chords, with a (somewhat obvious) predilection for minor chords. Adding the minor third into the power chord creates a much denser and more complex sound when played under heavy distortion. There are several reasons for this. To begin with, distortion accentuates each pitch's overtones, the upper frequencies that sound along with the main fundamental pitch and which give different instruments their distinctive sounds. In a power chord, the series of overtones of each pitch align with each other, contributing to its focused and forceful sound. Even in a major triad, the overtones remain clear and distinct. The minor chord, however, generates overtones that are in conflict with one another, introducing a lot of noise and dissonance (even though a minor triad is not itself dissonant). This phenomenon provides a good explanation for the relative lack of distorted minor chords in heavy metal from the 1970s and 1980s.[5] Black metal musicians, however, use distorted minor chords extensively, so they obviously like the tension and dissonance that these chords create.

These effects are further amplified when venturing beyond major and minor triads into diminished and augmented chords, or into extended harmonies like seventh and ninth chords. A visual illustration will be of assistance here, in this case using Overtone Analyzer, a software program that visualizes the overtones of particular sounds. The illustration below shows the series of overtones for a single note, a power chord, a major chord, a minor chord, an augmented chord, and finally a diminished chord, all played on a guitar with heavy distortion. The single note shows the overtone series for the root pitch of all these chords (E, played on the seventh fret of the A string in this case). The addition of the fifth to make a power chord adds more overtones, but they remain distinct from each other. The power chord also generates the subharmonic an octave below the root pitch. The overtones begin to get a bit more crowded with the addition of the major third, but they are still distinguishable. After this point, though, the series of overtones becomes more or less undifferentiated noise in the minor, augmented, and diminished chords. Augmented and diminished chords are especially noisy because they both avoid the use of a perfect fifth; augmented chords raise it a

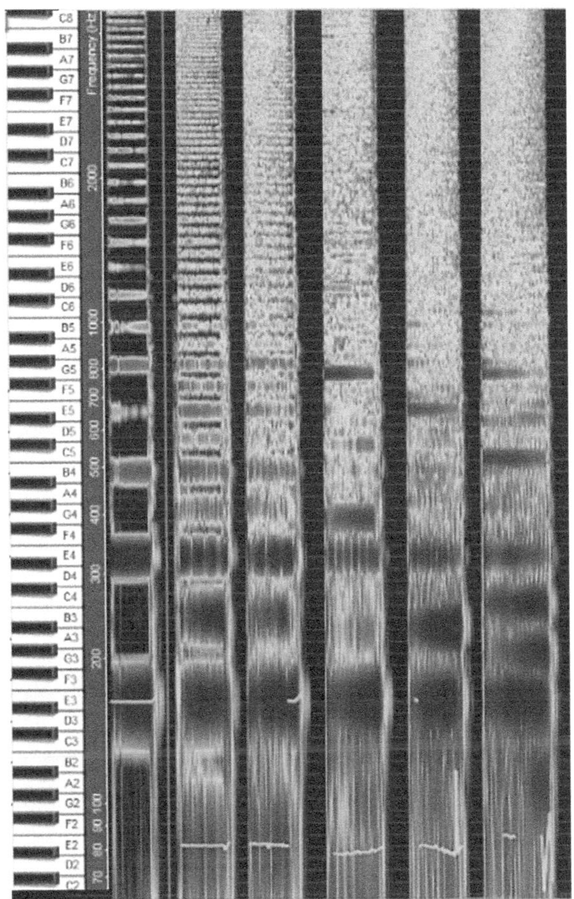

Example 3.2 *Overtone visualizations of guitar chords played with distortion. From left to right: Single note, power chord, major chord, minor chord, augmented chord, diminished chord.*

half-step while diminished chords lower it to create a tritone. It is also worth noting that the subharmonic originally generated by the power chord also becomes progressively "messier" and less distinct, especially for the diminished and augmented chords.

One of the striking things about being able to see the sounds in this manner is that the sonic noise of minor, diminished, and augmented chords becomes readily apparent. Single pitches, power chords, and major triads generate a clear series of overtones in each case, while the overtones of the other chords look almost like static. It also suggests that when black metallers describe a record as being "atmospheric" or "misty," this effect might have a lot to do with it, as these chords generate an awful lot of sonic "fog" around the fundamental pitches. Guitar distortion creates a lot of noise on its own even when playing single notes, assisted by the relentless fast picking employed by black metal guitarists, and utilizing chords just compounds the situation. The screamed and growled vocals of black metal create a similar effect, because they also utilize a much wider spectrum of frequencies than singing in definite pitches, generating similarly non-harmonic overtones.[6]

The way that black metal musicians use these chords also contributes to the music's sense of instability, particularly because the inclusion of the minor third creates a lot of potential for generating tritones or other dissonant intervals between different chords. As a result, black metal musicians have been particularly fond of pairing minor chords that they are either a minor third or major third apart, known as "chromatic mediants." For example, a C-minor triad (C-Eb-G) that moves up a minor third to Eb minor (Eb-Gb-Bb) includes a tritone motion between C and Gb, while moving up a major third to E minor (E-G-B) creates two half-steps between C/B and Eb/E.

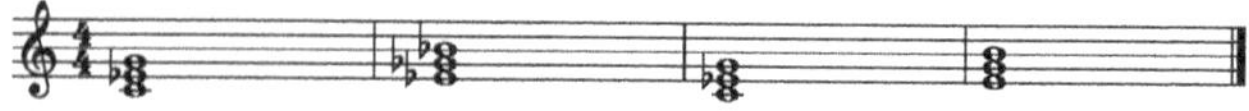

Example 3.3 *Chromatic mediant examples: C minor to Eb minor and C minor to E minor.*

In the world of diatonic music theory (the major/minor system typically taught in music classes), these kinds of progressions require significant envelope-pushing. Any sophomore music major should (hopefully) be able to tell you that in the key of C minor, the chord built on the E♭ should be a major triad, while an E minor triad wouldn't be an option at all because E is not in the C minor scale. Essentially, although the minor chord itself is a common musical entity, in this context it is used in a manner that violates the way it normally functions in traditional tonal harmony. As a result, these third-based chord movements create an odd sense of uncanniness and creepiness by making something familiar sound a little bit weird. Yet the progressions still retain a sense of consistency. In particular, the movement from C minor to E♭ minor retains E♭ as a common tone, while the move from C minor to E minor retains G as a common tone, which smooths the transitions between them. However, most guitarists approach these progressions of minor chords (or augmented and diminished chords for that matter) as chord shapes that are moved up and down the neck in parallel motion, rather than the smoother transitions desired in classical music. After all, metal is music that is written at the guitar, so the chords move in ways that are idiomatic to the instrument. Further, if one were to follow a long series of chromatic mediant motions, they very quickly arrive back at their starting point, as in Cm-E♭m-G♭m-Am-Cm in the minor third version and Cm-Em-A♭m-Cm in the major version. Essentially, minor chromatic mediant progressions build minor chords on the pitches of a diminished seventh chord while major mediants build minor chords on the pitches of an augmented triad, dividing the octave into four and three symmetrical divisions, respectively. There is not really a home pitch that articulates a "key" as defined in the major/minor system. Because of these qualities, chromatic mediants generate little in the way of momentum, feeling kind of directionless and wandering yet without introducing any jarring shifts or sonic clashes.[7]

In terms of how these kinds of ideas made their way into black metal, the French scholar Berenger Hainaut has made a convincing argument that black metal musicians came to love these kinds of chord progressions due to the influence of fantasy film scores from the 1970s and 1980s, which were themselves heavily influenced by nineteenth-century operatic and orchestral music.[8] Film composers like Bernard Herrmann, John Williams, Howard Shore, and Danny Elfman have regularly used these progressions of minor chords as signifiers for the fantastic and magical. It's not a particularly large leap to go from Williams's choir-heavy "Duel of the Fates" from *Star Wars: The Phantom Menace* or Elfman's theme for *Batman* to the more symphonic side of black metal pursued by Emperor, Dimmu Borgir, and many others.

Blackened Riffs

On *A Blaze in the Northern Sky*, Darkthrone rely almost exclusively on power chords, which makes sense given the fact that the album retains ideas from their death metal phase and that it hearkens back to older metal and punk. In the DVD for their *Preparing for War* boxed set, Fenriz describes the residual death metal elements as remaining out of necessity, due to the fact that their turn to black metal took place midway through the songwriting and demo process for their originally intended second album *Goatlord*.

They were therefore in a bit of a time crunch. Darkthrone don't really fully realize their conception of black metal until the following album *Under a Funeral Moon*, but there are moments in *A Blaze in the Northern Sky* that provide a preview of what's to come. In particular, the song "Where Cold Winds Blow" showcases two kinds of musical "gestures" that were to become hallmarks of Darkthrone's songwriting for their subsequent albums.

The opening riff of "Where Cold Winds Blow" is a tremolo-picked arpeggio that moves up and down across the lower three strings of the guitar, with each string left to ring out. The D string remains open. The lower two strings begin with a tritone on the third fret for G-C#-D, move up to a perfect fifth on the sixth fret for B♭-F-D, back to the original tritone, and then down to a perfect fifth on the second fret for F#-C#-D. Taken as a chord progression, we get something like Gsus(#4) - B♭maj – Gsus(#4) – Dmaj7 (in first inversion with no fifth). Depending on how the chords are voiced, these could almost sound jazzy, but Darkthrone take advantage of the open D to highlight the clashing minor second between C# and D, an interval that is otherwise rather difficult to create on a guitar.

Example 3.4 *Darkthrone, "Where Cold Winds Blow," opening riff.*

This sort of arpeggiated riff becomes a regular occurrence in Darkthrone's later albums. They use a similar idea in the main riff for "Natassja in Eternal Sleep" from *Under a Funeral Moon,* which maintains an open D string throughout while moving a major chord shape progressively higher on the neck, resulting in a similar series of different chord types. Comparable arpeggios make appearances in *Under a Funeral Moon's* second song, "Summer of the Diabolical Holocaust," and on the song "As Flittermice as Satans Spys" from *Transilvanian Hunger,* which obsessively arpeggiates a tritone for most of the song. In all of these cases, the bass part remains relatively static, simply repeating the lowest note of the arpeggio ad nauseam.

Although arpeggiated riffs like these were one of Darkthrone's signature gestures, they also became an important stylistic marker for Norwegian black metal in general. Snorre Ruch of the band Thorns is often credited with the development of this idea, along with black metal's penchant for minor chords and tritone relationships, all of which can be heard on Thorns's 1991 demo *Grymyrk.* The *Grymyrk* demo was initially only given out to the band's friends and consists only of guitar and bass without any drums or vocals, but it is regularly cited by Norwegian black metallers of that generation as a keystone of their musical style, highlighting the importance of these informal local networks. The tremolo-picked arpeggios in this music create a distinct effect, initiating a slowly undulating movement beginning on the lower strings before moving through several higher strings and then returning to the lowest pitch. The use of tremolo-picking further accentuates the sense of intense motion. Yet, the fact that riffs like these arpeggiate a single chord and that the notes are allowed to ring results in a single sustained harmony. Musically, these riffs function to impart rhythmic drive and flow to otherwise static or slower-moving harmonic progressions, rather like a grim version of the arpeggiated Alberti bass figure that was a common feature of eighteenth-century keyboard music.

This love of stasis and monotony also turns up elsewhere. About midway through "Where Cold Winds Blow," another one of Darkthrone's favorite musical gestures appears: riffs in which a lower string holds a single pitch while the notes change on one or two upper strings. Fenriz has referred to this as the "Bathory finger-moving technique,"[9] and it does indeed turn up in Bathory songs like "Call From the Grave" and "Chariots of Fire" from Bathory's *Under the Sign of the Black Mark* (1987), as well as on other albums. In the second riff of "Call from the Grave," for example, the fifth of an F power chord is moved up a half-step, creating an augmented fifth anticipating the F# power chord which follows shortly after.

While, in this case, Bathory uses this idea as a way to prepare the next chord, Darkthrone and their cohort seemed to like the monotonous effect that this technique could produce, even though there is still a sense of melodic motion. A number of Darkthrone's early black metal songs utilize this technique, with "Transilvanian Hunger" probably being the most famous. The main 2-measure riff of the song consists of a D-C-B-C

Example 3.5 *Bathory, "Call from the Grave."*

Example 3.6 *Darkthrone, "Transilvanian Hunger."*

melody played above an open A, alternating with a C-B-C-B phrase played over an E.

Beyond "Transilvanian Hunger," similar "finger-moving" riffs turn up in "En as I Dyke Skogen" from *Transilvanian Hunger*, as well as in "Inn I De Dype Skogens Fabn" and "To Walk the Infernal Fields" from *Under a Funeral Moon*, and in "The Pagan Winter" and "Where Cold Winds Blow" from *A Blaze in the Northern Sky*.

"Where Cold Winds Blow" actually contains three examples of this kind of riff. The first one is split between the guitar and bass; the bass holds an A for three beats while the guitar plays a tremolo-picked A-A♭-A figure over it. The other two riffs are in the mid-paced middle section of the song and involve ideas similar to Bathory's "Call from the Grave," in which an upper note in a power chord is either raised or lowered. In the first instance, shown below, the upper finger in an A power chord moves up a step to B and then walks chromatically back to A, followed by a G# power chord in which the upper octave is occasionally raised to A. The other "finger-moving" riff in this section simply alternates between a C-F# tritone and a C power chord.

For Darkthrone, I also imagine that part of the appeal of "finger-moving" riffs and tremolo-picked arpeggios lies in their

Example 3.7 *Darkthrone, "Where Cold Winds Blow," middle riff.*

inherent simplicity and economy of motion. When discussing riffs, Fenriz often self-deprecatingly refers to his limitations as a guitarist, but these sorts of riffs are also consistent with the black metal aesthetic that Darkthrone and their cohort were advancing. A lot of thrash metal and death metal riffs almost make more sense as finger exercises rather than melodies, and the black metal aesthetic intentionally dials that back. Musical complexity, both in riffs and rhythms, was a crucial part of the "heaviness" of death metal, but "finger-moving" riffs and simplistic arpeggios discard all of that in favor of relatively basic movements that nonetheless produce distinctive and grim-sounding results.

Finally, a number of black metal bands also make use of open strings on the guitar, allowing them to ring out even as chords change, heightening the tension and dissonance. The opening arpeggiated riff from "Where Cold Winds Blow" illustrates one approach. Doing this also blurs the distinctions between the chords somewhat. Another is the opening riff for Emperor's "With Strength I Burn" from *Anthems to the Welkin at Dusk* (1997), which opens with a strummed E minor chord followed by an arpeggiated tritone F# – low C – high C on the lower three strings. Meanwhile, the upper three open strings of the guitar continue to ring over this, creating a phantom C diminished/E minor polychord for a moment as the upper strings fade out. The use of open strings is a hallmark of much

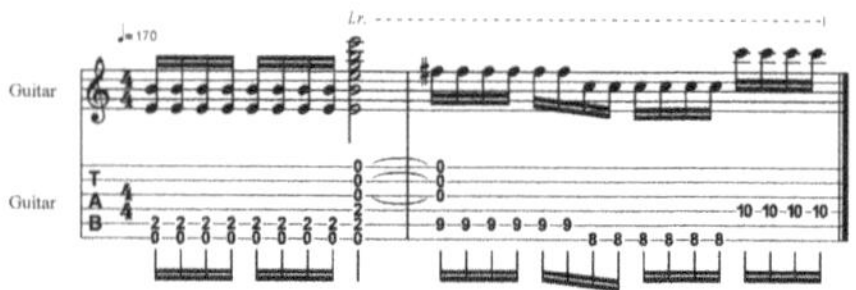

Example 3.8 *Emperor, "With Strength I Burn."*

music written at the guitar, but many black metal guitarists use them in service of introducing harmonic complexity and dissonance in addition to the more pragmatic way they are used by guitarists in other genres.

Blackened Rhythm

While thrash metal and death metal place individual and group virtuosity at the forefront of their music, the minimalism of black metal's distinctive musical components often makes performances into exercises in endurance. The guitar parts rely on relentless tremolo-picking, a technique that involves picking both up and down at very high speed in order to give the impression of a single sustained note that is interrupted by the articulations of the pick. The notes are never allowed to relax or decay, which results in a tense buzzing timbre. Although this sort of picking technique can be found in earlier thrash metal and death metal, black metal guitarists began using it not just for single notes and arpeggios but for full chords as well.

Similarly, black metal drummers often employ a technique called a "blast-beat," which involves intensely subdivided alternations between the kick and snare drum, basically a percussive equivalent to tremolo-picking. Taken together, these two techniques result in a constant barrage of sound.

However, these techniques also often seem to suspend forward motion since the rhythmic drive is muted somewhat without the clear articulations of the underlying beat. Darkthrone (in)famously took this monotonous and minimalistic approach to an extreme in *Transilvanian Hunger*, in which most of the songs sustain the same simplistic beat at approximately the same tempo with little in the way of fills or changes.[10]

As an example for comparison, let's consider the title track from Darkthrone's previous death metal album *Soulside Journey*. Over the course of four minutes and thirty-six seconds, "Soulside Journey" includes a dozen tempo changes, and nearly as many distinct riffs, although some riffs do reprise at later points. The song meanders like a river, as fast sections give way to drawn-out slow parts that suddenly pick up speed again. Even within single sections, musical variety is a primary concern, particularly for Fenriz, who often shifts his drum groove to half-time or double-time while the guitar parts continue to repeat the same riff. For example, the first riff of "Soulside Journey" is a fairly straight-forward 4-measure tremolo-picked chromatic figure, but Fenriz's drum part changes with each repetition, and even goes so far as to enter halfway through the first appearance of the riff. After two additional repetitions of the riff with shifts

Example 3.9 *Darkthrone, "Soulside Journey."*

between the hi-hat and ride cymbals, Fenriz changes to a half-time groove, another fairly standard move for death metal drummers.

Within genres like death metal and thrash metal, these sorts of complex and surprising musical changes are a large part of their appeal, and the numerous drastic shifts in "Soulside Journey" are standard features of early 1990s death metal. It was an integral part of Darkthrone's black metal aesthetic to discard these kinds of things in favor of a self-consciously "primitive" and simplistic rhythmic monotony as seen in *Transilvanian Hunger*.[11]

But, of course, *A Blaze in the Northern Sky* was only part of the way there, as some of the songs had been written prior to Darkthrone's decision to abandon their death metal style. As a result, some of the riffs in *A Blaze in the Northern Sky* retain the rhythmic characteristics of this earlier death metal material on *Soulside Journey* and the *Goatlord* demo, particularly in terms of the metric structure. For example, the first riff of "The Pagan Winter" uses a 16-beat structure, but instead of dividing it into four measures of 4/4, the middle two measures are a measure in 5/4 followed by one in 3/4. This introduces an internal asymmetry into a riff that otherwise conforms to normative phrase lengths, a device that is common in lots of death metal music, both then and now.

However, in this case, Fenriz tries to "blacken" the riff a little by playing a very "primitive" drum part with only a few fills and accents that follow the riff's changes. As the riff repeats and then reprises later in the song, he never alters the groove like in "Soulside Journey," although there is some variation in the fills. As a result, the sections sound relentless and relatively static, with little of the dynamism that characterized Darkthrone's earlier death metal style. The two versions of the song "A Blaze

Example 3.10 *Darkthrone, "The Pagan Winter."*

in the Northern Sky" also demonstrate this stylistic difference clearly. The original version recorded in the *Goatlord* sessions begins with slower sustained chords in one guitar while the second plays a melodic line and Fenriz plays a number of extended and elaborate drum fills to accent the chords. On *A Blaze in the Northern Sky*, however, they dispensed with the section's solo guitar melody entirely, played the underlying chord progression using tremolo-picking rather than letting the chords sustain, and Fenriz plays a constant blastbeat with few fills or cymbal accents. Although this approach certainly was successful in blackening this section without requiring revisions to the song structure, the original chord pattern's syncopated grooviness gets rather lost in it all. But that was undoubtedly the intention. Once Darkthrone was fully in the black metal world, however, they relied much more on balanced and symmetrical 2- and 4-measure riffs, as can be seen in the earlier examples. By eschewing rhythmic surprises and tempo shifts, they create the monotony and sense of stasis that was endemic to their conception of black metal's musical style.

Blackened Sound

For many listeners, the most immediately conspicuous aspect of *A Blaze in the Northern Sky* is its lo-fi "necro" sound. As has been well-documented, Peaceville Records was reluctant to release *A Blaze in the Northern Sky* without remixing it for a more professional sound. After all, Darkthrone's initial death metal album *Soulside Journey* embraced the mid-paced death metal style and polished production that was standard for other bands on the Peaceville roster. By all accounts, the label had little warning that their new Norwegian death metal band was about to go rogue. From Peaceville's perspective, *A Blaze in the Northern Sky* almost certainly sounded unfinished, like a cheap demo instead of a professional recording slated for release on one of the premier labels of the European extreme metal scene. The guitar tone in particular sounds brittle and fuzzy, without the sonic heft that typically accompanies metal guitar. The performances on the record sound more or less live, including feedback and guitar noises that would typically be edited out of the final mix. At times, the playing is also a little on the loose side as well. Yet for all its purposeful amateurism, I would argue that *A Blaze in the Northern Sky* is neither poorly produced nor poorly played. The guitar and bass tones are unorthodox for the time, but everything in the mix is well-balanced and easily discernible. However, there is a good chance that I might also just be well-accustomed to this particular kind of "necro" black metal sound, which enables me to pick out individual parts as I listen to *A Blaze in the Northern Sky* and similar-sounding albums.

With this in mind, it's worth a brief dive into what goes into the typical extreme metal recording, both currently and in the early 1990s, in order to appreciate the radical nature of Darkthrone's turn to the "necro" sound. Recording engineers who specialize in extreme metal face several challenges, particularly the need to create maximum heaviness without sacrificing sonic clarity. Mark Mynett's 2017 book *Metal Music Manual* details many of the standards and practices used today by recording engineers and producers who work with metal bands.[12] Because his book is intended for students currently studying music production, Mynett assumes the use of a digital audio workstation (DAW) program like ProTools as the primary recording medium. DAW programs have been the recording industry standard for decades, and one of their primary benefits is that the digital platform enables extensive editing of minuscule details. However, even before the arrival of computerized recording, it was common practice to compile a recording's final tracks out of multiple takes, sometimes going line-by-line in order to get the most perfect performance possible. In a DAW, however, this process can be done nearly as easily as cutting-and-pasting within a document file, with an undo button readily at hand.

The use of DAW recording also influences the way that individual instruments sound. In a twenty-first-century metal recording, guitars and basses are typically recorded on multiple tracks at once, capturing both the sound of a guitar amplifier and speaker cabinet (often using multiple microphones at different distances) and the unamplified direct signal from the instrument. This direct recording can then be used for "re-amping," in which the previously recorded guitar part is played through other amplifiers, digital amp simulators, or other effects. The final guitar tone heard on the recording is usually a blend of these sounds, which underscores the fact that the ideal recorded metal guitar tone is largely a studio construction. It is not without some irony that these composite tones are often praised for their naturalness.

Recording engineers also need to shape the tone of the sounds to improve the recording's overall clarity while retaining the heaviness and "bigness" of each instrument. The sound of the drums is of particular concern because extreme metal drumming can quickly become undifferentiated rumbling in the mix if the engineer uses the natural sound of the drums or opts for a big stadium-rock sound. Consequently, many extreme metal drummers prefer drum tones that are almost all attack with very little resonance and decay, which allows each individual drum hit to cut through the mix without covering up the other instruments. After all, extreme metal drummers are doing an awful lot of work, and they would understandably like it if listeners could hear what they're doing. However, using drum sounds that are all attack also risk making it sound like the drummer is playing a typewriter, so most engineers try to split the difference. In many cases, the sounds of the bass and snare drums are blended or entirely replaced with sampled drum sounds that are triggered by the drummer's playing, which allows for a uniform sound regardless of the natural fluctuations in the amount of force the drummer uses.

Beyond the ability to manipulate the sound and tone, the DAW environment also allows for the absolute regimentation of rhythm. Today, most metal recording sessions are done with a click track, which provides a master tempo for the musicians to follow. The tempos of the different sections are mapped out ahead of time, and the band will usually record songs section by section. Given the extreme performance demands of black metal and related styles, doing this makes sense. Otherwise, the later sections of the song might suffer due to fatigue. By using a click track, slight rhythmic imperfections in the performance can also more easily be put into sync because the recording engineer is able to work with musical subdivisions instead of seconds and milliseconds. If needed, individual notes can be moved or replaced, either one by one or through an automated process called "quantization" in which the DAW moves the sounds to sync up with subdivisions in the master tempo. As might be expected, doing this sacrifices the drummer's natural groove in the service of rhythmic precision. If a drummer has particularly sloppy footwork, they can even play to the click without using the bass drums at all, and then the engineer can compose the bass drum part from scratch using a sampled drum sound. In the end, many of the drum performances heard on extreme metal records today are human–computer hybrids, ranging from situations in which a few moments are time-corrected to those in which the drums are almost entirely programmed even though a human drummer is credited with the performance.

Given the importance of live performance in metal, many metalheads might be dismayed to know how much computerized intervention has likely taken place in some of their favorite records. Indeed, these kinds of rhythmic edits and sound replacements have been a part of extreme metal recording almost from the beginning. Jim Morris of the famous Morrisound Studios in Florida, known for pioneering recordings by Death, Cannibal Corpse, Obituary, and Morbid Angel in the early 1990s, has recounted how death metal drummers back then were often playing just beyond the edge of their abilities and often couldn't play along with a metronome.[13] As a result, maintaining steady tempos was a constant problem. Morris was recording on analog tape, so he ultimately developed a system involving time-code and a calculator to figure out how many milliseconds apart the bass drum hits needed to be. One of his assistants then had to input the replacement samples manually, one by one. Being able to do this task based on musical timing within a software program is obviously much more efficient, although it undoubtedly remains tedious work.

Morrisound quickly set the standard for death metal production in the early 1990s, and the recording engineer Scott Burns, in particular, crafted a template for recording death metal that yielded consistently effective results. In doing so, Burns and Morrisound created a readily identifiable sonic signature, and bands who recorded with them expected to get that sound. Then, as now, the economics of the music industry were a primary driver behind the use of studio techniques like drum replacement and standardized recording processes. These tools save expensive studio time that otherwise would be spent searching for unique guitar tones or trying in vain to get a perfect complete take of a challenging song. Yet, there is a certain irony in the fact that the restraints of finances and time resulted in amateurish, but unique-sounding, metal records in the early 1980s, but in the cases of Morrisound and most twenty-first-century metal production those same restraints result in numerous "professional"-sounding records that all sound basically alike.

In many respects, Darkthrone's recorded output from *A Blaze in the Northern Sky* onward has been an extended reaction against this increased standardization and professionalization. They certainly weren't alone in this; Euronymous went so far as to put a photo of Scott Burns inside a "no" symbol on the back cover of their 1993 reissue of the 1987 Mayhem EP *Deathcrush*.[14] Although "diss tracks" have had a long and storied life in popular music, I feel relatively confident stating that this is the only time a recording engineer has been publicly insulted in the artwork of an album he did not record, and by a band that he had possibly never even heard of. For *A Blaze in the Northern Sky,* Fenriz has described how their original bass player, Dag Nilsen (who was not officially in the band anymore but stayed on for the recording sessions), brought an expensive and "flashy" amp to the sessions but they instead had him play through a cheap Peavey amp with fuzz on it.[15] Darkthrone's thin and fuzzy guitar sound on *A Blaze in the Northern Sky* also serves as a reminder of what distorted electric guitars often sound like in real life when they aren't augmented by layering and re-amping. Ted recalls that the guitars were recorded by running their Marshall heads into a Gorilla amplifier, a cheap practice amp with a 6.5 inch speaker.[16] It's a clear homage to the low-budget sound of early Bathory and Hellhammer but done intentionally instead of simply happening out of necessity or incompetence. The local studio Darkthrone used, Creative Studio in Kolbotn, had hosted Mayhem for the recording of their *Deathcrush* EP in 1987. Although the members of Mayhem have recalled that the engineer had no idea how to record their kind of music and just sort of set things up and let them go, Fenriz has said that the technician at Darkthrone's session several years later did a good job. It's not clear if it was the same engineer for both sessions, but in both cases the bands describe just bashing the music out live with a minimum of overdubbing or other edits. Indeed, Ted has recalled that he hadn't even rehearsed black metal vocals prior to their recording session, and just had to figure it out in the booth and hope for the best.[17]

While Darkthrone turned to a deliberately "primitive" kind of sound, some of the bands in their circle began exploring other sorts of unorthodox sound aesthetics. In particular, the records produced by Eirik Hundvin (aka Pytten) at Grieghallen in Bergen often feature a distinctly spacious sound due to the fact that the drums and guitars were recorded on the stage of the Grieghallen opera house. This sound is famously showcased in Mayhem's *De Mysteriis dom Sathanas* and Emperor's *Anthems to the Welkin at Dusk,* both of which are cloaked in reverberation. However, these records sound the way they do not because of a lack of resources but rather because they purposefully utilized a resonant acoustic space designed for the performance of opera and classical music. Younger black metal bands like Paysage d'Hiver, Velvet Cacoon, and Darkspace have cultivated even more opaque and murky productions, in which the ear strains to locate individual parts within the mix, adding to the aura of mystery surrounding the music.[18] Compared to recordings like these, it might make sense to consider whether *A Blaze in the Northern Sky* could be better described as "mid-fi," a concept put forth by the musicologist Mei-Ra St-Laurent to describe metal recordings in which the mix is well-balanced, "punchy," and clear in spite of the relatively raw and "live" sound.[19]

Darkthrone's rejection of the clarity and precision cultivated by other metal records also suggests to the listener that their recordings are intended to be heard as a literal "record" of a performance, rather than a painstakingly refined studio product. In the years since their first black metal records, Darkthrone have continued to cultivate these markers of amateurism as indicators of authenticity and realness, inviting listeners to imagine that we are simply hearing them play through their songs in real time. Since *Transilvanian Hunger,*

Darkthrone have largely recorded in their own home studio and they seem to follow their original ideal of recording the music quickly and without much fussing about. A series of cartoons printed in Germany's *Legacy* magazine as a part of the promotional push for Darkthrone's 2010 album *Circle the Wagons* illustrated the band's writing and recording process, including Fenriz laughing at the prospect of a second take of his drum parts.[20] Whether or not that dedication to "one and done" is exaggerated in the service of comedy, it's clearly the ideal they are promoting. While Darkthrone obviously take care in dialing in the kinds of sounds they want, and their existence as a duo means that there must be a fair bit of overdubbing in order to create the full metal ensemble, their ideal result remains one with a minimum of editing or other mediation.

In the end, there is perhaps a small irony that this music which has such a reputation for misanthropy began as a reaction against the *dehumanization* of metal music production. Beneath all the grim rhetoric, Darkthrone's vision of black metal is one in which the "humanity" of the music is a point of pride, grounded in the sonic experience of humans playing metal music in the real world, and celebrating the imperfections that come from that. But this is perhaps simply yet another ironic contradiction in a scene that is rife with them. For example, black metal musicians express their yearning for a pre-modern world by making music dependent on modern technology, and they espouse radically individualistic philosophies while their music is directly and indirectly subsidized by the collectivist ideals underpinning Nordic social democracies. Even metal music itself, broadly speaking, is a musical style supposedly opposed to commercialism that nonetheless thrives within the corporate music industry. In any case, the creation of the "necro" black metal sound by Darkthrone and others forged a new metal aesthetic by invoking the past, albeit one that had been mostly ignored and forgotten. As we'll see in the last chapter, the retro impulse that initially drove the creation of *A Blaze in the Northern Sky* still remains at the heart of Darkthrone's musical aesthetic in the twenty-first century.

4 "The Pagan Winter"

What is your opinion on the blackmetal [sic] scene these days, is there anything missing?

Fenriz: I care about metal in general, and I like the raw bands with the old sound. Anything newer sounding (production) than 1987 is completely uninteresting to me, but more importantly I am mainly looking for metal up to 1985 now, newer bands that play these styles are also very interesting, like Atomic Roar from Brazil, Nocturnal from Germany, Deathhammer from Norway etcetera.[1]

In 2015, I had the opportunity to attend the Blekkmetal festival in Bergen, a three-day black metal and tattoo festival organized by Ivar Bjørnson of Enslaved, the logo and tattoo artist Jannicke Wiese-Hansen, and production coordinator Kirsti Rosseland. In addition to nostalgically minded sets by Bergen bands like Enslaved, Aeternus, Kampfar, Gaahl's Wyrd, Taake, and Helheim, the festival also featured tattoo artists, horror film screenings, art exhibitions, and live interviews and panel discussions about the Bergen black metal scene. The festival's goal was, in their words, to "turn back the time to before 1994, to the old mood, the old feeling, the art, the people, the bands," and in this spirit it was kept relatively small and the bands waived their usual performance fees, taking any payment in free tattoos. The bands were of course fantastic, but my interest was especially piqued by the panel discussions, which featured members of Kampfar and Hades, the record producer Eirik "Pytten" Hundvin, and Finn Bjørn Tønder, the Bergen journalist whose interviews with Varg Vikernes first connected the arsons and murder of Magne Andreasson to the black metal scene. With the exception of Tønder's final panel, none of the panels made more than passing references to the crimes that made their scene internationally infamous, which at first seemed to me like they were ignoring a rather large elephant in the room. Upon further reflection, though, it made some sense that this would be the case given the festival's nostalgic focus on the genre's halcyon days, when "Norwegian black metal" was still mostly a loose collection of teenage metalheads playing in their parents' garages while writing letters and trading tapes back and forth with each other. All weekend I couldn't quite shake the feeling that I had essentially flown across the Atlantic to attend a high-school reunion, but one where they watch *Der Todesking* and listen to Pytten discuss recording *De Mysteriis dom Sathanas* instead of engaging in awkward small talk. Under those circumstances, it seems natural that older attendees and performers might not want to dwell on those in their cohort who turned their glory days upside down. It's much more fun to relish the gauzy nostalgia of remembering more innocent exploits and shenanigans with a live soundtrack of music from their teenage years.

Recently, Darkthrone has seemingly become a similar vehicle in which Fenriz and Nocturno Culto get to re-experience and recreate the music of their youth. Beginning with their 2006 album *The Cult Is Alive,* Darkthrone began a new creative era that focused less on the black metal style in favor of 1980s hardcore punk, speed metal, and thrash metal. As put by Aquarius Records in their review of *The Cult Is Alive*, "the cult sounds less black than ever, and instead like the heaviest, most kick-ass eighties hardcore band you've never heard."[2] Although the "primitive" black metal of their first albums was obviously also looking to the past for inspiration, Darkthrone's twenty-first-century music wears nostalgia on its sleeve. It has become perhaps less a matter of Darkthrone being influenced by 1980s punk and speed metal, and more that Darkthrone are simply writing 1980s-style punk and speed metal songs. To this end, the initial social media marketing for their 2019 album *Old Star* promised that the album sounds "like the 80s never left," and it pretty much lives up to that claim. Darkthrone's lyrics in this new phase also began to include pithy self-referential jabs at twenty-first-century metal itself, including such gems as, "You call your metal black? It's just plastic, lame, and weak!" from "Too Old, Too Cold" (2006) and "I am the Graves of the 80s / I am the risen dead / Destroy their modern metal / And bang your fucking head!" from the 2010 song "I am the Graves of the 80s." Although these lines are objectively funny for metalheads, I'd argue that their humor also carries a deeper truth that Darkthrone want to convey.

As Darkthrone made this stylistic shift to earlier styles, metal as a whole in the 2000s and 2010s was undergoing a turn towards revivalist nostalgias. For example, a number of 1980s thrash bands that had either disbanded or explored other musical styles in the 1990s reunited and/or attempted to return to their thrash roots, including major names like Metallica, Slayer, Exodus, and Megadeth. These years also saw the arrival of a new generation of younger thrash metal bands like Municipal Waste and Toxic Holocaust. The prolific music writer Simon Reynolds posits a more general twenty-first-century cultural trend towards reunions, remakes, mash-ups, tributes, and other sorts of commemorations in his book *Retromania*.[3] He makes the point that although earlier eras have always found inspiration in the past, there's a difference between reaching back to a bygone era versus obsessing over the products of only twenty years ago. Reynolds's concept of retromania echoes a number of other conceptions of the current cultural moment, in which the Internet-fueled abundance of past products has compressed the past into the present, creating a flattened and fragmented view of history in which everything seems to exist at once without context. At the very least, over the past generation the Internet has allowed the past to begin haunting the present in ways that it was not able to do previously.[4] It might not be entirely hyperbolic to suggest that the idea of "loss" is itself in danger of being lost. A rather paradoxical side effect is that music and films that never made the jump to digital or online formats might wind up being doubly lost because we've essentially forgotten that we've forgotten them. Under such circumstances, nostalgic revivalism might be understood not only as a desire to return to the past, but also a desire to be reassured that the past existed in the first place.

This need for rootedness and connection extends to geography, because the Internet also excels at collapsing distance as well as time. As music listening and consumption takes place increasingly in online spaces, locating bands geographically has become ever more valuable as a means of establishing identity and context. As such, a self-exoticized "tourist" kind of presentation can come to the fore for bands from around the world, or at least those with international ambitions. While the Norwegian black metal scene of the 1990s promoted their local identity as a way to assert themselves in the face of increasing globalization, in the twenty-first century it seems as if the foregrounding of locality has also become a key function *of* globalization. As the earlier exploration of black metal's promotion of geographic isolation and wilderness demonstrated, and as real estate agents have always known, location does function as a form of capital, even just symbolically. Certainly, if one considers "Norwegian black metal" to be an intentional form of branding (as I do), it bears comparison with other sorts of national and regional brandings like "German engineering", "Scottish whisky," or "Kansas City BBQ." For metal music and other products, those national labels carry a lot more symbolic weight beyond simply telling consumers where a band or other product originated. They invite listeners to engage with a deeper narrative about that particular country and its culture, regardless of whether it is based in reality or even constructed intentionally.[5] Under these circumstances, the idea of "local" becomes romanticized as inherently subversive and authentic, in opposition to the anonymous homogenizing forces of globalization, particularly if the local culture in question can claim a distinct identity based on ethnicity or language.[6]

Although the global/local divide is not by any means a simple dichotomy, perhaps especially in cases of local music scenes that command a global audience and that cultivate connections with other local scenes, it remains a powerful symbolic organizer for many music fans. Even if the Internet has made geographic location almost meaningless in terms of determining access to particular music for those of us with reliable high-speed connections, it seems that we still like our music to be from *somewhere*. This ideal perhaps holds especially true when that actual geographic location has been wrapped in centuries-deep layers of exoticized cultural fantasies, as is the case with Norway and the Atlantic North in general. As we've seen, these conceptions are important both for Norwegian black metal's global listenership and for the musicians themselves.

Naturally, it should also be noted that metal bands from places like Latin America, Africa, Southeast Asia, and the Middle East certainly experience the effects of globalization in different ways. They also have to interact with the social, religious, and political situations that are unique to their particular location, and their music is conceived in response to those conditions and in ways that might be completely lost on listeners abroad. While at one point this might have been simply a story of metal traveling from the West to these locations via imported cassettes, then being taken up and replicated by metal fans there, the situation has engendered a vast multitude of cultural flows and interpretations that are beyond this slim volume.[7]

For black metal, as with similar musical styles, the loss of the comparative obscurity afforded by time and distance has had far-reaching effects that underpin its turn to nostalgia. Of course, black metal fans of my generation are old enough to remember when finding this music required digging through whatever was available in local record stores or trying to find zines and mailorder catalogs. For fans like me who lived outside of big cities or college towns, black metal and other kinds of underground music were pretty hard to locate, or even know about. In searching for this music, we'd pore over CD liner notes, lists of shout-outs to other bands, the few zines we might find, and write to the labels for catalogs. Even if one did know about some particular band or recording, it might not have been possible to obtain, particularly for fans who weren't plugged into tape (and later CD-R) trading networks. Indeed, *A Blaze in the Northern Sky* and Darkthrone's other albums with Peaceville were rather difficult to find in the United States prior to a series of reissues in the early 2000s. In my case, all I heard of Darkthrone's music from the mid-1990s until probably the mid-2000s was the song "A Blaze in the Northern Sky" as included on the *Peaceville 4* compilation CD, which I randomly found in a used record store. Now, of course, it's possible to plug into a never-ending stream of black metal from any era and from all around the world. If I want to hear, for example, the 1994 demo *Sogneriket* by the Norwegian band Windir, I can instantly call it up on YouTube despite the fact that the band only made about ten copies of it (and whichever copy of the tape wound up being digitized also sounds like it got damaged at some point or was just a bad dub to begin with). Similarly, sites and services like YouTube, Spotify, MySpace (RIP), and especially Bandcamp host the music of thousands of black metal bands from around the world. As delightful as it can be to browse through so many of these bands, it can also become rather overwhelming, even if that's a good problem to have. I also must admit that my own musical activities are actively adding to this landfill of amateur black metal that nobody asked for.[8] Along with the musical obscurities, black metal zines are also being archived by several sites like Jason Netherton's Send Back My Stamps, along with zine anthologies published by Cult Never Dies, Bazillion Points and other publishers.[9] For scholars and fans alike, there is an impressive archive being created.

With such a vast amount of material at one's fingertips, it's perhaps not surprising that the touchstones of the past generations become increasingly important for listeners, and the metal music industry obviously recognizes the profit potential of this kind of nostalgia. Many of black metal's foundational albums have reached their twentieth and twenty-fifth anniversaries, and bands like Mayhem and Emperor accordingly presented album play-through sets at festivals and tours in 2017–18. Long-running bands, including Darkthrone, have released limited-edition vinyl reissues and retrospective boxed sets, some costing several hundreds of dollars even before they hit the resale market. These expensive items also clearly seem to be a response to the current popularity of vinyl collecting and the relative absence of continuing income from streaming or CD sales. Indeed, vinyl reissues have become an important revenue stream for the music industry in general, so much so that independent labels and musicians often find their new releases backlogged at the limited number of still-functioning record presses. For fans, however, these boxed sets especially may function more as status items rather than records they regularly spin. My experience may not be universal, but I can say that I almost never listen to the few of these that I own; they're basically the musical equivalent of collectible figurines in their original packaging. Beyond reissues, limited editions, and boxed sets, there is also a robust collector's market for actual black metal ephemera and rarities. For example, an original copy of Burzum's 1993 EP *Aske*, which had as its cover art a photo of the burned Fantoft stave church and a very limited run of lighters featuring the same image, can fetch several thousand dollars even without the lighter. If the highlighting of metal bands' national identities demonstrates a desire for rootedness in locality, there's a clear argument that the collecting drive reflects a concurrent desire for the physicality of tapes, CDs, records, patches, and so forth.

Beyond commercialized nostalgia and collecting, the metal music industry has also grown immensely since Darkthrone's early career. As only one example, the long-running German metal label Century Media was acquired by Sony Music in

2015 for $17 million. The twenty-first century has also seen the growth of an extensive network of metal festivals across Europe and in the Americas, showcasing both extreme metal and more mainstream fare. In continental Europe, the largest and most famous are probably Wacken Open Air in Germany and Hellfest in France, which has built a permanent facility in the middle of French wine country that includes a Ferris wheel, in-house food service, and Hell City, which is basically a metal version of Disneyland's Main Street USA, with Jägermeister and Harley-Davidson gear instead of candy and soda shops. These weekend-long festivals feature multiple stages, dozens of bands, and have essentially become pilgrimage sites for metal fans from across the globe, attracting upwards of 50,000 attendees per day. In the summer, metal fans with the time and financial resources could easily spend months festival-hopping across the continent. Beyond the festivals, the touring circuit in continental Europe has also grown extensively. This expansion was facilitated in no small measure by the creation of the Eurozone and the Schengen Area in 1999, which made it much easier and less expensive to mount European tours by doing away with the need for work visas, customs clearances, and import duties on merchandise. Not incidentally, those things remain significant bureaucratic and financial barriers for European bands trying to book tours in the USA, while musicians in the UK watched the Brexit situation unfold with much anxiety and alarm for the same reasons. The sudden months-long suspension of live music events around the world in response to the coronavirus outbreak in Spring 2020 will also likely have long-lasting effects in this vital sector of the music industry. As of this writing, bands, promoters, and venues already face potentially massive losses and debts as a result of canceled tours and festivals, and many of their futures remain uncertain.

The underground and countercultural nature of black metal is also undoubtedly in question, given that black metal music, patches, and other merchandise are easily found on eBay, Amazon, Etsy, and in Hot Topic stores. The Adult Swim cartoon *Metalocalypse* certainly assisted greatly in this regard by making black metal more visible in the United States, even as it parodied extreme metal culture and aesthetics for a much wider audience. One effect of this wider availability is that the subcultural currency of black metal ephemera like patches and shirts has been diminished, since owning them no longer necessarily reflects one's dedication to the scene.[10] As with earlier countercultures like the hippie movement and punk, black metal's clearly defined artistic aesthetic and its emphasis on amassing collections of records, shirts, and patches for "battle jackets" and vests makes it particularly vulnerable to this kind of diffusion. If at one point these patches and shirts meant that a fan had seen a particular band, or was just "in the know" enough to find such products, those products' usefulness as subcultural status symbols necessarily fades somewhat now that they can often be easily purchased without much fuss. The metal battle jacket is fashioned after those traditionally worn by biker gangs (themselves modeled on military regalia), in which patches and pins indicate earned ranks and other specific achievements. Metalheads currently treat them more as a personally curated display of one's tastes, which of course generates its own value by demonstrating the wearer's individuality while simultaneously declaring their allegiances. However, I have noted that some metal fans have begun adorning their vests not only with patches but also with the fabric entry bracelets now used at festivals, so that they once again illustrate the wearer's specific metal experiences.

Black metal's visual and fashion aesthetic has also proven to be fertile ground for artists, illustrators, and cosplayers, taking a place alongside gothic, cyberpunk, and steampunk fashions. A search for the tag #blackmetal on the amateur art website DeviantArt brings up all manner of things, including models in fetish garments, portraits of black metal musicians, and cartoon anthropomorphic animals wearing corpsepaint and spiked gauntlets. Fenriz is a popular subject as well, inspiring both realistic portraits and cute anime-style illustrations. For example, in 2015, Fenriz served a term as a town councilman in the village of Oppegård, although he attempted to not be elected by making posters of himself holding his cat with the caption "Please do not vote for me," and a note at the bottom stating that the ad was "paid for by Cats for Fenriz." His efforts failed and he was elected, because apparently in Norway it is not possible to withdraw from one's civic duty if nominated for such a post. But his poster inspired a number of fan artists.

Black metal's reach sometimes extends into stranger places, as with the vaporwave artist Transilvanian Hunger,

Example 4.1 *Parody of Fenriz's anti-election poster, refashioned into a city ID card, by John-Ross Boyce, 2019. Used by permission.*

who borrowed Darkthrone's album title as a moniker for their unsettling plunderphonic collages made from processed samples of obscure elevator music and 1980s yacht rock. Norwegian black metal has also definitively entered the self-aware world of Internet memes. The band Immortal and their singer/guitarist Abbath in particular have inspired a number of goofy looping gifs, underlining the potential for campiness that lurks beneath black metal's grim aesthetic. As is the way with memes, they can quickly go down the proverbial rabbit hole. For example, a friend recently sent me a looping gif of the Pokémon Squirtle dramatically donning sunglasses with the caption, "Big sunglasses, cool band," a reference to a drunken video interview Fenriz gave in 2011. In the interview, he pointed out the sunglasses worn by the singer of the obscure Los Angeles thrash band Détente on the back cover of their 1986 album *Recognize No Authority*, and quipped, "Big sunglasses = cool band."[11] I got the meme reference immediately, and I suspect many other Darkthrone fans would as well, even though explaining it in writing obviously takes a bit of work. Varg Vikernes of Burzum even briefly became a YouTube celebrity of sorts, posting video monologues about black metal, survivalism, white nationalism, and role-playing games, until his channel was deleted in a purge of white nationalist and neo-Nazi users. He even had a little catchphrase ("Let's find out!") that made its way onto t-shirts and meme images. Further, black metal parodies and mash-ups abound, including black metal-style logos for pop stars like Lady Gaga and Katy Perry, along with inspired and hilarious music video parodies like "Black Metal Barbie" and "Norwegian Reggaeton." Another popular YouTube video features a dad in full black metal garb and corpsepaint entertaining his young daughter by building a church out of popsicle sticks and then burning it. As noted by Michelle Phillipov, videos of metal dads and similarly "grown-up" products like metal-themed cookbooks or Youtube cooking shows reimagine being "metal" as something that could include domestic and parental duties as well, although the incongruities make for some good chuckles.[12]

Black metal has also occasionally popped up in legitimate advertisements for various products, including a Canadian ad for Kentucky Fried Chicken, although in most cases the black metal aesthetic is used as a foil for parody and humor. In a slightly different vein, the American post-black metal band Deafheaven was featured in 2016 as part of series of musically focused short Youtube films funded by the Ray-Ban sunglasses brand. Although this development mirrors the increasingly common alliances between indie rock musicians and corporate advertising agencies, the campaign focused on Deafheaven's artistic defiance against the conformity of "true" black metal.[13] Regardless of how one feels about Deafheaven or the imperative of "trueness" in black metal culture, there is a certain irony about a band using a corporate platform to argue for their own originality against the norms of an underground music subculture.

Ultimately, these situations work to clarify the limits of black metal's transgressive and dangerous side.[14] Obviously, the criminal element of Norwegian black metal could not continue to be a driver of the scene, even if many of the musicians and visual artists employing the black metal aesthetic continue to highlight and profit from its associations with real-world violence.[15] The members of Mayhem seem to feel this paradox particularly keenly, because their successful performing and recording career in the twenty-first century rests partly on the graves of their deceased members, Per "Dead" Ohlin and Øystein "Euronymous" Aarseth. The bassist Necrobutcher, especially, seems to feel a lot of survivor's guilt regarding Ohlin in particular.[16] For fans, however, the violence of the past has largely become the stuff of fantasy, a fading memory for those old enough to remember it and a distant point in history for younger generations. It seems reminiscent of fascinations with killers like Charles Manson and Ted Bundy or Old West outlaws like Billy the Kid; the intervening years obscure the brutality and destructiveness of their crimes and replace them with a veneer of romanticized notoriety. To this end, the merch table at the Salt Lake City date of Mayhem's 2017 tour featured a particularly cheeky T-shirt with a stylized graphic of a church silhouetted by flame with the caption "Burn Your Local Church." The turn to nostalgia seems in some ways like a natural response to both the abundance of new black metal and the desire to escape the more troubling aspects of the genre's past via winking parodies or by revisiting it in a different light, as seen in the Blekkmetal festival. There's also admittedly been more than a little of that impulse at work in the writing of this book.

These sorts of changes in the scene's subcultural meanings and values are also responses to the fact that the original fans of underground metal are getting older, and these fans now approach their participation in the scene in different ways. In particular, looking "metal" or otherwise competing for status within a music scene likely seems much less important or appealing for many older fans.[17] Attendance at gigs and festivals often becomes a matter of choosing one's battles because of increased work and family responsibilities, but in some cases also in terms of minding one's health and physical safety. For metalheads with disabilities or chronic health concerns, engaging with the scene in bars or other concert venues may not be possible at all. The life of a touring metal musician is also often one of instability and financial difficulty, even for fairly well-known performers, and musicians who want to raise families may find that goal to be incompatible with their music careers.

That said, there is always something a little subversive and countercultural about identifying with a past generation, if only as a means of rhetorically escaping from the confines of modernity and mass culture. This impulse can be seen at work repeatedly in popular music, from 1960s folk musicians' looking to the blues and "hillbilly" recordings of the 1930s, to the creation of "classic rock" in the early 1980s, to the Bathory-inspired riffs of *A Blaze in the Northern Sky*. Metal music has in some ways always been about exploring these sorts of alternatives to mundane reality, whether that might involve occult and horror topics, science fiction, ancient legends and myths, biker subcultures, or simply the experience of being "metal." At a time when metal is more abundant and available than ever, it's perhaps not that surprising that metal might seek to escape into its own mythologized past as well.

"The Final Superjoint Ritual ... We Are a Blaze in the Northern Sky"

If one looks into various histories of music, art, and literature, it becomes clear that one of the implied agendas of these histories is usually to advance a particular narrative of artistic progress via a limited list of Great Works that either build upon or subvert their predecessors. In music, this kind of trajectory is clearly evident in the standard repertoire of European classical music, but it also organizes many popular histories of jazz and rock music. There's a standard arc that culminates in an aesthetic "Golden Age" that retroactively organizes the entire enterprise, with everything preceding the style's supposed apex conceived in the terms of its future development, while later works are almost inevitably cast as failures of one sort or another as the style falls into decadence, degradation, and repetition. In histories of classical music, the Golden Age revolves around Vienna in the late eighteenth and early nineteenth centuries, jazz histories privilege either the genre's apex of mass popularity in the 1930s and 1940s or its subsequent artistic turn in bebop, while rock history tends to revolve around the latter half of the 1960s and especially the career of The Beatles.

Although these sorts of stylistic narratives have been questioned for decades within academia, they prove incredibly resilient, and indeed the "three waves" model of black metal's development continues to hold sway over the conception of black metal's life as a musical style. This view of black metal history certainly underpins the commercialized nostalgia driving much of the industry. It's so pervasive that it's honestly hard to conceive of the genre's history in any other way; even arguing that the "second wave" retroactively created the notion of a "first wave" doesn't escape the model. But even if Darkthrone and their circle remain a crux point for black metal, as I think they should, the question of what to do with the following generation still seems up for debate. Returning to the comparisons with "world music," and also drawing from my own individual experience as a black metal musician, I think it's worth considering that black metal's musical aesthetics can function in a similar fashion to types of traditional music, even though it remains a commercial enterprise. As theorized by Philip Bohlman, traditional music is by nature recursive rather than progressive; tradition is never used up or relegated to the past but is continually restored in the present, accruing new meanings along the way.[18] Conceived in this way, revivalist or "retro" musical styles do not necessarily signal the death of originality or progress, because there's no longer a need for a linear trajectory and originality is no longer an essential virtue. Darkthrone's career beginning with *A Blaze in the Northern Sky* has been marked by repeated returns to the "Graves of the 80s," as they put it, so it makes perfect sense for Darkthrone to leapfrog backwards over the musical style they helped to create and go back to the older music that originally inspired them.

It is perhaps this recursive quality within black metal music and culture that has helped to endear Darkthrone to generations of black metallers, although there is maybe one last distinctly Nordic component at play. Within Scandinavian cultures, there is a stereotypical tendency to value humility, consensus, and community at the expense of individuality. This ideal was famously parodied in the 1930s by the Danish author Aksel Sandemose, who coined the term "Jante Law" after his fictional Danish town Jante.[19] This code essentially states that as a member of the community you are not to brag or think yourself better than anyone else, with the implied threat that you will be put in your place if you do so. It is similar to the "tall poppy" idea found in other parts of the world, which likewise discourages arrogance and overachievement. Black metal's emphasis on individualism and the general music industry imperative of self-promotion are obviously at cross-purposes with this sentiment, but I think it does explain a few things about Darkthrone's place within the world of black metal and their lack of engagement with the show business side of the music industry. Although I obviously can't psychoanalyze

Ted and Fenriz, I think it is fair to say that much of their career has been marked by a dislike of spectacle, or at least an ambivalence towards it.

Darkthrone's aversion to live performance is one of the central aspects of their career, and has also allowed them to avoid many of the trappings of show business. In a memoir by Peaceville Records founder Paul "Hammy" Halmshaw, Fenriz describes a trip to London to visit the label as the only flight he has ever taken, and he comes off as potentially a little phobic about air travel.[20] Luckily, black metal is welcoming of the "studio-only" band in a way that many other metal styles are not, thanks to a long history of bands that exist as one or two musicians on record, but which have never been a performing ensemble. Darkthrone is one of many black metal bands, including Bathory and Burzum, who exist purely as songwriting and recording units and who feel no obligation to ever hit the stage, for a variety of reasons. It bears some comparison with the massive success of Swedish and Norwegian pop songwriters and producers, who have written and produced dozens of massive hits for American pop stars while maintaining relatively low profiles.

This sense of humility extends to other interactions with the media. Fenriz in particular has become something of an evangelist for underground and classic metal, curating radio shows and putting together a truly massive Spotify playlist of favorite metal songs as a part of the promotional drive for Darkthrone's 2019 album *Old Star*. In interviews and media appearances, Fenriz regularly expounds on the music he loves by playing songs for his guests, thumbing through records and noting which ones have particularly good drum or guitar sounds, extolling the virtues of Uriah Heep, complaining about modern record production, and so forth.

In an appearance on a Norwegian morning variety show, he took the host on one of his favorite hikes through the forest and barely discussed music at all. This ethos extends to Darkthrone releases themselves. Tellingly, the 2014 Darkthrone boxed record set *Black Death and Beyond* has as its spine graphic the spines of five other records: Bathory's *Blood Fire Death* (1988), Dark Angel's *Darkness Descends* (1986), Accept's *Breaker* (1981), Destruction's *Infernal Overkill* (1985), and Klaus Schulze's *Timewind* (1975). It's worth noting that *Blood Fire Death* is the only "black metal" record listed; Accept's *Breaker* sounds a lot like Judas Priest; Dark Angel and Destruction are oft overlooked 1980s thrash metal bands; and *Timewind* is a classic record of electronic space music. A retrospective boxed set is basically the height of artistic self-importance, but the spine's design works to deflect attention away from Darkthrone. While boxed sets and other large record albums usually stick out on record shelves because of their size, *Black Death and Beyond* hides in your record collection by disguising itself as five other LPs, some of which you might already own. If you don't own them, obviously Darkthrone think you should.

Darkthrone's lack of rock-star ambitions and genuine nerdiness about metal has done much to endear them to black metal fans all over the world, because in a lot of ways Darkthrone are basically just like many of their their fans. Even though Darkthrone are paragons of black metal music, they still work regular day jobs and seem perfectly happy doing so. Essentially, Ted and Fenriz seem to live largely unremarkable mundane lives while writing and recording their music as time and inspiration allow. In this, they are much like the millions of metal fans and musicians around the world who balance their metal activities against their work and family responsibilities.

The only difference is that Darkthrone are among the primary architects of their musical genre, and their recordings have been enjoyed by millions of fans. But even then, Fenriz might prefer to redirect your attention to some super-obscure thrash metal demo from the 1980s that you absolutely, positively have to hear.

Notes

Introduction

1   The 1990/91 rehearsal tapes for *Goatlord* were released
by Moonfog Productions in 1996, with vocal parts
that Fenriz had overdubbed in 1994. The instrumental
versions were released on the *Frostland Tapes* compilation
with Darkthrone's other demos from the late 1980s by
Peaceville Records in 2008. Darkthrone, *Goatlord*, Moonfog
Productions, FOG 013, 1996, compact disc; Darkthrone,
Frostland Tapes, Peaceville Records CDVILEB243, 2008, three
compact discs.

2   Edward W. Saïd, *Orientalism* (New York: Pantheon Books,
1978).

3   Darcy Steinke, "Satan's Cheerleaders," *Spin*, February 1996,
62–70.

4   Among many others, see Laina Dawes, *What Are You
Doing Here?: A Black Woman's Life and Liberation in Heavy
Metal* (Brooklyn, NY: Bazillion Points, 2012); Amber Clifford,
Queerness in Heavy Metal Music: Metal Bent (New York:
Routledge, 2015); Pauwke Berkers and Julian Schaap,
Gender Inequality in Metal Music Production (Bingley, UK:
Emerald Publishing, 2018); Rosemary Hill, *Gender, Metal
and the Media: Women Fans and the Gendered Experience
of Music* (London: Palgrave Macmillan, 2016); and Florian
Heesch and Niall Scott, *Heavy Metal, Gender and Sexuality:
Interdisciplinary Approaches* (New York: Routledge, 2016).

5   Laura Wiebe, "Nordic Nationalisms: Black Metal takes Norway's Everyday Racisms to the Extreme," in *Reflections in the Metal Void*, ed. Niall W. R. Scott (Oxford: Inter-Disciplinary Press, 2012), 185–97.

6   Benjamin R. Teitelbaum, *Lions of the North: Sounds of the New Nordic Radical Nationalism* (Oxford: Oxford University Press, 2017); Benjamin R. Teitelbaum, "Collaborating with the Radical Right: Scholar-Informant Solidarity and the Case for an Immoral Anthropology," *Current Anthropology* 60, no. 3 (June 2019): 414–35.

7   *Once Upon a Time in Norway*, dir. Pål Aasdal and Martin Ledang (Oslo: Grenzeløs Productions, 2007), on Youtube.com, https://www.youtube.com/watch?v=uX7QTv_Zvpo.

Chapter 1

1   Ian Reyes, "Blacker than Death: Recollecting the 'Black Turn' in Metal Aesthetics," *Journal of Popular Music Studies* 25, no. 2 (June 2013): 244.

2   Vladimir Nabokov, *Invitation to a Beheading*, trans. Dmitri Nabokov (New York: Vintage International, 1989), 26.

3   Andrew Zierlyn, liner notes to *Black Death and Beyond*, Peaceville EBVILE004, 2014, three LPs.

4   Dayal Patterson, *Black Metal: Evolution of the Cult* (Townshend, WA: Feral House, 2013), 194.

5   Woodrow Steinken, "Norwegian Black Metal, Transgression, and Sonic Abjection," *Metal Music Studies* 5, no. 1 (2019): 21–33.

6   Benjamin Hillier, "The Aesthetic-Sonic Shift of Melodic Death Metal," *Metal Music Studies* 4, no. 1 (March 2018): 5–23.

7   Jason Arnopp, "We Are but Slaves of the One with Horns ..."
     Kerrang!, March 27, 1993, 42–6.

8   Stanley Cohen, *Folk Devils and Moral Panics: The Creation of
     the Mods and Rockers*, 3rd ed. (1972; New York: Routledge
     Classics, 2011).

9   There is also a strong argument that these hearings mark
     the beginning of the academic study of heavy metal, both
     in terms of scholars examining its connection to crime and
     delinquency and scholars attempting to defend it against
     the PMRC's attacks. See Jeffrey Arnett, *Metalheads: Heavy
     Metal Music and Adolescent Alienation* (Boulder: Westview
     Press, 1996) and Robert Walser, *Running with the Devil:
     Power, Gender, and Madness in Heavy Metal Music* (Hanover,
     NH: Wesleyan University Press, 1993), 137–71.

10   Michael Moynihan and Didrik Søderlind, *Lords of Chaos: The
     Bloody Rise of the Satanic Metal Underground* (Venice, CA:
     Feral House, 1998), 171–90.

11   Steinken, "Norwegian Black Metal"; Nick Richardson,
     "Looking Black," in *Black Metal: Beyond the Darkness*, ed. Tom
     Howells (London: Black Dog Publishing, 2012), 149–59.

12   Keith Kahn-Harris, "Beyond Transgression: Breaking Metal's
     Boundaries" (lecture, Boundaries and Ties: The Place of
     Metal Music in Communities, University of Victoria, June 9,
     2017).

13   Julian Fox, "Ashes Against the Grain: Black Metal and the
     Grim Rebirth of Romanticism," in *Rock and Romanticism:
     Post-punk, Goth, and Metal as Dark Romanticisms*, ed. James
     Rovira (London: Palgrave Macmillan, 2018), 240.

14   Dick Hebdige, *Subculture: The Meaning of Style* (London:
     Routledge, 1979).

15   Ibid., 96.

16   Ibid., 96–9.

17   Matt Hills, *Fan Cultures* (New York: Routledge, 2002), 27–30.

18   See David Muggleton and Rupert Weinzerl, eds. *The Post-Subcultures Reader* (New York: Berg, 2003); Andy Bennett and Keith Kahn-Harris, eds. *After Subculture: Critical Studies in Contemporary Youth Culture* (New York: Palgrave Macmillan, 2004); Howard S. Becker, *Art Worlds* (Los Angeles: University of California Press, 1982); Michael Maffesoli, *The Time of the Tribes: The Decline of Individualism in Mass Society* (London: Sage, 1996).

19   J. Patrick Williams, *Subcultural Theory: Traditions and Concepts* (Cambridge: Cambridge University Press, 2011), 124–5.

20   Deena Weinstein, "Rock's Guitar Gods – Avatars of the Sixties," *Archiv für Musikwissenschaft* 70, no. 2 (2013), 143.

21   Ibid., 143–4.

22   Keir Keightley, "Reconsidering Rock," in *The Cambridge Companion to Pop and Rock*, eds. Simon Frith, Will Straw, and John Street (Cambridge: Cambridge University Press, 2001), 109–42.

23   Ibid., 137.

24   Ibid., 125–30.

25   It is also worth noting the religious connotations of the term "kvlt," both in terms of a "cult" as a religious movement and its eventual adoption as a media term, along with its connection to "occult," referring to secret or hidden knowledge. For further exploration of religiosity as a part of media fandoms and subcultures, see Matt Hills, *Fan Cultures* (New York: Routledge, 2002), 117–30; Robin Sylvan, *Traces of the Spirit: The Religious Dimensions of Popular Music* (New York: New York University Press, 2002).

Chapter 2

1   Noctir, "My Flesh Yearns … for the Tombworld: Review of Darkthrone – A Blaze in the Northern Sky," *Encycolpedia Metallum*, September 7, 2008, https://www.metal-archives.com/reviews/Darkthrone/A_Blaze_in_the_Northern_Sky/612/Noctir/123274.

2   Evil_Johnny_666, "Unleashing the Storm: Review of *A Blaze in the Northern Sky*," *Encyclopedia Metallum*, January 14, 2011, https://www.metal-archives.com/reviews/Darkthrone/A_Blaze_in_the_Northern_Sky_-_Preparing_for_War%3A_Vol._1/454344/.

3   Toni-Matti Karjalainen, "Tales from the North and Beyond: Sounds of Origin as Narrative Discourses," in *Sounds of Origin in Heavy Metal Music*, ed. Toni-Matti Karjalainen (Newcastle upon Tyne: Cambridge Scholars Publishing, 2018), 1–41.

4   Borealist exoticism is of course not limited to music, and scholars in various fields have considered the concept under several related terms, including Thisted's "Arctic Orientalism," "Nordicité" as theorized by Louis-Edmond Hamelin and Daniel Cartier, and "Nordientalism." I am relying on "borealism" because it already has gained some usage within studies of Nordic music. Kirsted Thisted, "De-framing the Indigenous Body: Ethnography, Landscape and Cultural Belonging in the Art of Pia Arke," *Nordlit* 29 (2012): 279–98; Louis-Edmond Hamelin, *Discours do Nord* (Quebec: Université Laval, 2002); Daniel Chartier, "Towards a Grammar of the Idea of North: Nordicity, Winterity," *Nordlit* 22 (2007): 35–47; Hans Hauge, *Post-Danmark: Politik og æstetik hinsides det nationale* (Copenhagen: Lindhardt & Ringhof, 2003).

5   The history of the indigenous Inuit and Sámi cultures in the North is also a part of the story of borealism, particularly because it more closely mirrors the patronizing and discriminatory legacy of colonialism elsewhere in the world.

6   Philip Bohlman, "Musical Borealism: Nordic Music and European History," 33–55; Kimberly Cannady, "Echoes of the Colonial Past on Discourse on North Atlantic Popular Music," 203–21; Tony Mitchell, "Music and Landscape in Iceland," 145–62 in *The Oxford Handbook of Popular Music in the Nordic Countries*, eds. Fabian Holt and Antti-Ville Kärjä (New York: Oxford University Press, 2017).

7   Sigur Rós, *Sigur Rós: Heima*, dir. Dean DeBlois (London: EMI Records, 2007), DVD.

8   Joshua Green, "From the Faroes to the World Stage," in *The Oxford Handbook of Popular Music in the Nordic Countries*, 111–29.

9   Bohlman, "Musical Borealism," 40–1.

10   Green, "From the Faroes," 111.

11   Christopher Thompson, *Norges Våpen: Cultural Memory and Uses of History in Norwegian Black Metal* (Uppsala: Acta Universitatis Upsaliensis, 2018), 151–91.

12   Timothy Taylor, *Music and Capitalism: A History of the Present* (Chicago: University of Chicago Press, 2015), 89–92.

13   Simon Frith, "The Discourse of World Music," in *Western Music and Its Others: Difference, Representation, and Appropriation in Music*, eds. Georgina Born and David Hesmondhalgh (Oakland: University of California Press, 2000), 307.

14   Enslaved, *Vikingligr Veldi*, Deathlike Silence Productions, Anti Mosh 008, 1994, compact disc; Ulver, *Bergtatt*, Head Not Found, HNF 005, 1995, compact disc.

15   Ralph Waldo Emerson, *Nature* (Boston: James Munroe and Company, 1836), https://archive.org/stream/naturemunroe00emerrich#page/n5/mode/2up.

16   Edmund Burke, *A Philosophical Inquiry into the Origin of Our Ideas of the Sublime and Beautiful* (Oxford: Oxford University Press, 1990).

17   Ross Hagen, "Ideology and Mythology in Norwegian Black Metal," in *Metal Rules the Globe: Heavy Metal Music around the World*, eds. Harris Berger, Paul Greene, and Jeremy Wallach (Durham, NC: Duke University Press, 2011), 180–99.

18   Thompson, *Norges Våpen*, 166–91.

19   Kevin Hoffin, "Decay as a Black Metal Symbol," *Metal Music Studies* 4, no. 1 (2018): 81–94. Black metal bands like Xasthur and Shining who dwell on themes of mental health, suicide, and isolation often explore similar ideas of dissolving one's consciousness, but from a rather different perspective.

20   Dean Swinford, "Black Metal's Medieval King: The Apotheosis of Euronymous through Album Dedications," in *Medievalism and Metal Music Studies: Throwing Down the Gauntlet*, eds. Ruth Barratt-Peacock and Ross Hagen (Bingley, UK: Emerald Press, 2019), 121–37.

21   Thompson, *Norges Våpen*, 201.

22   Teitelbaum, *Lions of the North*, 2017.

23   Kennet Granholm, "'Sons of Northern Darkness': Heathen Influences in Black Metal and Neofolk Music," *Numen* 58, no. 4 (2011): 514–44; Kennet Granholm, "Ritual Black Metal: Popular Music as Occult Mediation and Practice," *Correspondences* 1, no. 1 (2013): 5–33.

24 Henna Jousmäki, "Christian Metal and the Translocal North," in *The Oxford Handbook of Popular Music in the Nordic Countries*, 131–43; Caroline Lucas, Mark Deeks, and Karl Spracklen, "Grim up North: Northern, England, Northern Europe and Black Metal," *Journal for Cultural Research* 15, no. 3 (2011): 279–96.

25 Zygmunt Bauman, "From Pilgrim to Tourist – or a Short History of Identity," in *Questions of Cultural Identity*, eds. Stuart Hall and Paul Du Gay (Thousand Oaks, CA: SAGE Publications, 1996), 29–30.

26 Jakob Stougaard-Nielsen, "Nordic Noir in the UK: The Allure of Accessible Difference," *Journal of Aesthetics and Culture* 8, no. 1 (2016), https://doi.org/10.3402/jac.v8.32704.

27 Gianluca Chelini, "Javanese Black Metal: Towards a Definition of Post-Heritage Music," in Sounds of Origin in Heavy Metal Music, ed. Toni-Matti Karjalainen (Newcastle upon Tyne: Cambridge Scholars Publishing, 2018), 95–117.

28 For more in-depth examples, see Thomas Burkhalter, *Local Music Scenes and Globalization: Transnational Platforms in Beirut* (New York: Routledge, 2013).

Chapter 3

1 Ian Reyes, "Blacker than Death: Recollecting the 'Black Turn' in Metal Aesthetics," *Journal of Popular Music Studies* 25, no. 2 (June 2013), 240–57.

2 Ibid., 254.

3 Glenn Pillsbury, *Damage Incorporated: Metallica and the Production of Musical Identity* (New York: Routledge, 2006).

4 I might note that melodic tritones are not limited to sounding "evil"; like everything in music it all depends on context. For example, the song "Maria" in Leonard Bernstein's *West Side Story* uses a tritone motif that sounds yearning and lyrical, although the later callback of the motif in "Cool" highlights the tritone's tension and conflict, which relates directly to the musical's plot and to Maria's situation in particular. "Cool" also references tritones' crucial role in the harmonic language of jazz and blues music. Beyond this, melodic tritones can sound dreamy and hazy in the hands of Debussy, make Henry Mancini's *Pink Panther* theme sound (ironically) sly and sneaky, and pass by almost entirely unnoticed in Danny Elfman's theme for *The Simpsons*.

5 Esa Lilja, *Theory and Analysis of Classic Heavy Metal Harmony* (Helsinki: IAML Finland, 2009); Esa Lilja, "Dealing with the 3rd: Anatomy of Distorted Chords and Subsequent Compositional Features of Classic Heavy Metal," in *Modern Heavy Metal: Markets, Practices and Cultures International Academic Research Conference, June 8–12, 2015, Helsinki, Finland: Proceedings*, eds. Toni-Matti Karjalainen and Kimi Kärki (Helsinki: Aalto University & Turku: International Institute for Popular Culture, 2015), http://iipc.utu.fi/MHM/Lilja2.pdf

6 Marcus Erbe, "By Demons Be Driven: Scanning 'Monstrous' Voices," in *Hardcore, Punk, and Other Junk: Aggressive Sounds in Contemporary Music*, eds. Eric James Abbey and Colin Helb (Lanham, MD: Lexington Books, 2014), 51–72.

7 For a truly deep dive into this arena of music theory, see Richard Cohn, *Audacious Euphony: Chromaticism and the Consonant Triad's Second Nature* (Oxford: Oxford University Press, 2012).

8 Berenger Hainaut, "'Fear and Wonder': Le fantastique somber et l'harmonie des médiantes, de Hollywood au black metal," *Volume!* 9, no. 2 (2012): 179–96.

9   Fenriz, "Interview: Fenriz," interviewed by Todd Nief, *Invisible Oranges*, April 16, 2013, http://www.invisibleoranges.com/interview-fenriz/.

10   It is worth noting, however, that most black metal drummers continue to subtly emphasize the underlying meter during blast-beat sections in performance, using dynamic accents or cymbals, if only to make sure that the rest of the band doesn't lose track of where "1" is. Fenriz's monotonous playing on *Transilvanian Hunger* is a bit of an outlier in that regard, enabled by the fact that he was overdubbing all the other instruments himself and there was no intention of ever playing the songs live.

11   Given Fenriz's omnivorous musical tastes, I also can't help but wonder if there's some influence from krautrock bands like Can, whose drummer Jaki Liebezeit pursued a similarly minimalistic "motorik" rhythm in his playing.

12   Mark Mynett, *Metal Music Manual: Producing, Engineering, Mixing, and Mastering Contemporary Heavy Music* (New York: Routledge, 2017).

13   Jason Netherton, *Extremity Retained* (London, ON: Handshake Inc., 2014), 219–21.

14   Mayhem, *Deathcrush*, Deathlike Silence Production, Anti-Mosh 003, 1993, compact disc.

15   Peaceville Records, "Darkthrone – The Interview – Chapter 2: A Blaze in the Northern Sky (from Preparing for War boxset)," video, 13:50, November 7, 2011, https://www.youtube.com/watch?v=-5E3gHlAJxA.

16   Andrew Zierlyn, liner notes to *Black Death and Beyond*, Peaceville EBVILE004, 2014, three LPs.

17   Andrew Zierlyn, *Black Death and Beyond*.

18   There has also been some crossover between black metal and avant-garde noise music, such as Wold, Wolf Eyes, and Abruptum, in which black metal's musical elements are combined with sonic walls of electronic feedback and noise.

19   Méi-Ra St-Laurent, "'It's kind of in the middle': The 'Mid-Fi' Aesthetic: Toward a New Designation of Black Metal Aesthetic of Recording. The Case of the Québec Black Metal Scene," in *Proceedings of the 12th Art of Record Production Conference: Mono: Stereo: Multi*, ed. Jan-Olof Gullö (Stockholm: Royal College of Music & Art of Record Production, 2019), 267–86.

20   Nagawika, "Darkthrone: Circle the Wagons," https://freeyourmindzine.files.wordpress.com/2013/02/germany-legacy.jpg.

Chapter 4

1   Fenriz, "Darkthrone – 28/11/2007," interviewed by Eugene Straver and Thomas van Golen, *Metal-Experience.com*, http://www.metal-experience.com/interviews/Interview%20Darthrone%202007.htm.

2   This quote was from the Aquarius Records' notably extensive and detailed online catalog, which is unfortunately no longer publicly available after the store's closure. I owe thanks to the store's former proprietor Andee Connors for personally sharing all their old Darkthrone reviews with me.

3   Simon Reynolds, *Retromania: Pop Culture's Addiction to Its Own Past* (New York: Faber and Faber, 2011).

4   For more on the "hauntedness" of the late twentieth and early twenty-first centuries, see Jacques Derrida, *Specters of Marx, the State of the Debt, the Work of Mourning, & the New International*, trans. Peggy Kamuf (New York: Routledge,

1994) and Mark Fisher, *Ghosts of My Life: Writings on Depression, Hauntology and Lost Futures* (Zero Books, 2014).

5   Toni-Matti Karjalainen, "Tales from the North and Beyond: Sounds of Origin as Narrative Discourses," in *Sounds of Origin in Heavy Metal Music*, ed. Toni-Matti Karjalainen (Newcastle upon Tyne: Cambridge Scholars Publishing, 2018), 1–41.

6   Ian Biddle and Vanessa Knights, "Introduction – National Popular Musics: Betwixt and Beyond the Local and Global," in *Music, National Identity and the Politics of Location*, eds. Ian Biddle and Vanessa Knights (Farnham: Ashgate, 2007), 1–15.

7   See for example, Nelson Varas-Diaz, *The Metal Islands: Culture, History, and Politics in Caribbean Heavy Metal Music*, video, 1:37:25, October 27, 2017, https://www.youtube.com/watch?v=6awhR7X57o4; Edward Banchs, *Heavy Metal Africa: Life, Passion, and Heavy Metal in the Forgotten Continent* (Tarentum, PA: Word Association Publishers, 2016); Jeremy Wallach, Harris M. Berger, and Paul D. Greene, eds. *Metal Rules the Globe: Heavy Metal Music around the World* (Durham, NC: Duke University Press, 2011).

8   Keith Kahn-Harris, "Landfill Metal: The Ironies of Mediocrity," in *Modern Heavy Metal: Markets, Practices and Cultures International Academic Research Conference, June 8–12, 2015, Helsinki, Finland: Proceedings*, eds. Toni-Matti Karjalainen and Kimi Kärki (Helsinki: Aalto University & Turku: International Institute for Popular Culture, 2015), http://iipc.utu.fi/MHM/Kahn.pdf.

9   http://sendbackmystamps.org; http://www.cultneverdies.com; Jon Kristiansen, *Metalion: The Slayer Mag Diaries* (New York: Bazillion Points, 2011).

10 Ross Hagen, "Kvlt-er than Thou: Power, Suspicion, and Nostalgia within Black Metal Fandom," in *The Ashgate Research Companion to Fan Cultures*, eds. Linda Duits, Koos Zwaan, and Stijn Reijnders (Burlington, VT: Ashgate, 2014), 227–30.

11   Walvisleuter, "Fenriz interview for Rockhard magazine,"
      video, 10:00, May 1, 2007, https://www.youtube.com/
      watch?v=Bh2-MeMuDul.

12   Michelle Phillipov, "Hamburgers of Devastation: The
      Pleasures and Politics of Heavy Metal Cooking," *International
      Journal of Community Music* 7, no. 2 (2014): 259–72.

13   Jeffrey S. Podoshen, "Constructing Black Metal Mythology
      for Global Monopoly: #ittakescourage," *Metal Music Studies*
      4, no. 2 (2018): 375–80.

14   Keith Kahn-Harris, "Beyond Transgression: Breaking Metal's
      Boundaries" (lecture, Boundaries and Ties: The Place of Metal
      Music in Communities, University of Victoria, June 9, 2017).

15   Michelle Phillipov, "Extreme Music for Extreme People?
      Norwegian Black Metal and Transcendent Violence," *Popular
      Music History*, vol. 6, no. 1/2 (2011): 150–68.

16   Jørn Stubberud, *The Death Archives: Mayhem 1984–94* (New
      York: Ecstatic Peace Library, 2018).

17   See Andy Bennett, "Punk's Not Dead: The Continuing
      Significance of Punk Rock for an Older Generation of Fans,"
      Sociology 40, no. 2 (2006): 219–35; Paul Hodkinson, "Ageing
      in a spectacular 'youth culture': Continuity, Change, and
      Community amongst Older Goths," *The British Journal of
      Sociology* 62, no. 2 (2011): 262–82.

18   Philip Bohlman, *World Music: A Very Short Introduction*
      (Oxford: Oxford University Press, 2002).

19   Askel Sandemose, *A Fugitive Crosses his Tracks* (New York:
      A. A. Knopf, 1936). It's worth noting that Jante Law may
      have taken on a life of its own as a sort of self-fulfilling
      prophecy among Scandinavians.

20   Paul Halmshaw, *Anything for a Peaceville Life* (Hell Segundo,
      2016).

Index